CW00508383

Jane Eyre

A play

Willis Hall

Adapted from the novel by Charlotte Brontë

Samuel French — London
New York - Toronto - Hollywood

© 1994 BY WILLIS HALL PRODUCTION (book and lyrics)
AND STEPHEN WARBECK (music)

Rights of Performance by Amateurs are controlled by Samuel French Ltd, 52 Fitzroy Street, London W1T 5JR, and they, or their authorized agents, issue licences to amateurs on payment of a fee. **It is an infringement of the Copyright to give any performance or public reading of the play before the fee has been paid and the licence issued.**
The Royalty Fee indicated below is subject to contract and subject to variation at the sole discretion of Samuel French Ltd.

Basic fee for each and every
performance of the play by   Code M
amateurs in the British Isles

Basic fee for each and every
performance of the music by   Code A
amateurs in the British Isles*

The Professional Repertory Rights in this play are controlled by SAMUEL FRENCH LTD, 52 Fitzroy Street, London W1T 5JR.
The Professional Rights, other than Repertory Rights, are controlled by ALEXANDRA CANN REPRESENTATION, 337 FULHAM ROAD, LONDON SW10 9TW.

* The use of the music is mandatory

The publication of this play does not imply that it is necessarily available for performance by amateurs or professionals, either in the British Isles or Overseas. Amateurs and professionals considering a production are strongly advised in their own interests to apply to the appropriate agents for written consent before starting rehearsals or booking a theatre or hall.

ISBN 978 0 573 01802 2

Please see page vi for further copyright information

JANE EYRE

First presented at the Crucible Theatre, Sheffield, on the 5th of November, 1992, with the following cast:

Jane Eyre	Emma Fielding
Mr Brocklehurst/Mason/Porter	Richard Howard
Lord Ingram/Reverend Wood/St John Rivers	Peter Lindford
Rochester	Jack Shepherd
Bessie/Country Girl/Orphan Girl/Kitty	Charlotte Barker
John Reed/Groom/Manservant/Briggs/Builder	Simeon Defoe
Helen Burns/Adele/Mary Rivers	Susan Gardner
Grace Poole/Lady Ingram/Hannah	Pauline Jefferson
Mrs Reed/Bertha Rochester/Shopkeeper	Valerie Lilley
Miss Temple/Blanche Ingram/Diana Rivers	Shona Morris
Miss Abbot/Mrs Fairfax/Countrywoman	Maggie Wells
Eliza/Leah/Barbara/Mary Ingram/Orphan Girl	Gillian Wright

Directors Robert Delamere and Michael Rudman
Designer Fran Thompson
Music Stephen Warbeck
Musical Direction Sarah Homer and Anna Hernery
Musicians Sarah Homer and Anna Hemery

COPYRIGHT INFORMATION

(See also page ii)

This play is fully protected under the Copyright Laws of the British Commonwealth of Nations, the United States of America and all countries of the Berne and Universal Copyright Conventions.

All rights including Stage, Motion Picture, Radio, Television, Public Reading, and Translation into Foreign Languages, are strictly reserved.

No part of this publication may lawfully be reproduced in ANY form or by any means—photocopying, typescript, recording (including video-recording), manuscript, electronic, mechanical, or otherwise—or be transmitted or stored in a retrieval system, without prior permission.

Licences for amateur performances are issued subject to the understanding that it shall be made clear in all advertising matter that the audience will witness an amateur performance; that the names of the authors of the plays shall be included on all programmes; and that the integrity of the authors' work will be preserved.

The Royalty Fee is subject to contract and subject to variation at the sole discretion of Samuel French Ltd.

In Theatres or Halls seating Four Hundred or more the fee will be subject to negotiation.

In Territories Overseas the fee quoted above may not apply. A fee will be quoted on application to our local authorized agent, or if there is no such agent, on application to Samuel French Ltd, London.

VIDEO RECORDING OF AMATEUR PRODUCTIONS

Please note that the copyright laws governing video-recording are extremely complex and that it should not be assumed that any play may be video-recorded for whatever purpose without first obtaining the permission of the appropriate agents. The fact that a play is published by Samuel French Ltd does not indicate that video rights are available or that Samuel French Ltd controls such rights.

CHARACTERS

John Reed
Jane Eyre
Bessie
Miss Abbot
Mrs Reed
Mr Brocklehurst
A Groom, at Gateshead Hall
Miss Temple
Helen Burns
Barbara, a maid
A Nurse
Mrs Fairfax
A Porter
Leah, a housemaid
Adele
Grace Poole
Edward Rochester
Kitty, a housemaid
John, a man-servant
The Dowager Lady Ingram
Lord Ingram
Mary Ingram
Blanche Ingram
Richard Mason
Bertha Mason
The Reverend Wood
Briggs, a solicitor
Shopkeeper
Country Girl
Country Woman
Diana Rivers
Mary Rivers
Hannah
St John Rivers
Annie
Alice
A Builder
Narrators, School children, Guests, Carol-singers, *etc*.

SYNOPSIS OF SCENES

ACT I

	Prologue
Scene 1	The Red Room, Gateshead Hall
Scene 2	The Drawing Room, Gateshead Hall
Scene 3	The Driveway, Gateshead Hall
Scene 4	A Classroom, Lowood School
Scene 5	Miss Temple's Apartment
Scene 6	The Sick Room, Lowood School
Scene 7	Outside St Stephen's Church, Lowood
Scene 8	Jane's Bedroom, Lowood School
Scene 9	Thornfield Hall
Scene 10	A Country Lane
Scene 11	Thornfield Hall
Scene 12	The Garden, Thornfield Hall
Scene 13	Rochester's Bedroom
Scene 14	The Gallery
Scene 15	The Ballroom, Gorstone Hall
Scene 16	The Drive, Thornfield Hall
Scene 17	Thornfield Hall
Scene 18	Thornfield Hall
Scene 19	The Garden, Thornfield Hall
Scene 20	Jane's Bedroom, Thornfield Hall

ACT II

Scene 1	Thornfield Hall
Scene 2	The Church, Thornfield
Scene 3	Bertha Mason's Chamber
Scene 4	The Garden, Thornfield Hall
Scene 5	Thornfield Hall
Scene 6	The Parlour, Moor House
Scene 7	The Girl's School, Morton
Scene 8	The Parlour, Moor House
Scene 9	A Moorland Glen, near Morton
Scene 10	Outside Thornfield Hall
Scene 11	The Garden, Ferndean

AUTHOR'S PRODUCTION NOTE

In the original staging, at the Crucible Theatre, Sheffield, the play was given an ensemble production with a cast of twelve players all of whom (with the exception of Jane and Rochester) doubled several parts. Reference to the original cast list on a preceding page will show how this can best be effected. The play could, of course, also be produced with a larger company and without recourse to doubling. Also, in the original production, the children at both Lowood School and at Morton Girls' School were played by the members of the company— some societies may care to consider using children for these scenes.

The narrative passages, representing the voice of Jane Eyre, were also distributed among the entire cast (again with the exception of Rochester) sometimes entering in unison, sometimes positioned separately around the stage. The numbering of the Narrators' speeches throughout the script is not intended as a guide to casting — as the actor or actress playing the role of First Narrator in the first scene, for example, need not be expected to take the same role in a subsequent scene. It is recommended that, once the casting of the play's characters is completed, the distribution of the Narrators' speeches would be best effected in rehearsal, scene by scene, in order to take into account the availability of the cast at any given moment during the play.

Fran Thompson's ingenious setting for the original production, on the Crucible's thrust stage, incorporated a line of black, Gothic pillars supporting a gallery playing area which was accessible by a flight of stairs. As this edition is based, principally, on the original staging, there are constant references to this gallery. Smaller societies however, whose resources or stage contours preclude the building of a "gallery", should in no way allow this fact to dissuade them from staging their own production — the scenes played on the gallery could equally be accomplished on a lower level.

Indeed, the near cinematic style of this dramatization demands that the scenes flow easily into one another, and without pause — to which end, the scenery should be minimal. The play could, in fact, be performed on an otherwise bare stage with the furniture and props required: a few chairs; a blackboard; some small tables; a bed, etc., carried on and off (or pre-set) whenever possible by the actors and actresses themselves, rather than by stage-management. What is important to the early-nineteenth century feel of any production, is the close, claustrophobic sense produced by small acting areas contained in pools of candlelight.

It is recommended that the piano remain on stage throughout the play and that the pianist and or musicians be dressed in costume to blend with the period of the play.

Willis Hall

Other plays by Willis Hall published by Samuel French Ltd

Christmas Crackers
Kidnapped at Christmas
The Long and the Short and the Tall
The Play of the Royal Astrologers
The Railwayman's New Clothes
A Right Christmas Caper
Treasure Island (musical, adapted from R. L. Stevenson)
Walk On, Walk On
The Water Babies (musical, adapted from Charles Kingsley)
The Wind in the Willows (musical, adapted from Kenneth Grahame)

Other plays by Willis Hall and Keith Waterhouse published by Samuel French Lt

All Things Bright and Beautiful
Billy Liar
Celebration
Children's Day
Say Who You Are
Sponge Room *and* Squat Betty
Who's Who
Whoops-a-Daisy
Worzel Gummidge

ACT I

As the House Lights fade there is the sound of a strong wind soughing over the Yorkshire moors. As the wind dies away, some half-dozen or so members of the Company, acting as Narrators and the voice of Jane Eyre, enter in phalanx and in measured tread

First Narrator There was no possibility of taking a walk that day.

Second Narrator We had been wandering indeed, in the leafless shrubbery an hour in the morning——

Third Narrator — the cold winter wind had brought with it clouds so sombre, and a rain so penetrating——

Fourth Narrator — that further outdoor exercise was now out of the question.

Fifth Narrator I was glad of it; I never liked long walks.

Sixth Narrator Dreadful to me was the coming home in the raw twilight, with nipped fingers and toes——

First Narrator — and a heart saddened by the chidings of Bessie, the nurse, and humbled in the knowledge that I was plain while my cousins Eliza and Georgina Reed were pretty.

Second Narrator John, their brother, was four years older than I, for I was but ten.

Third Narrator He bullied and punished me; not two or three times in the week, nor once or twice a day but continually:

Fourth Narrator — every nerve I had feared him, and every morsel of flesh on my bones shrank when he came near.

Over which, one of the Company steps out of the phalanx, becoming John Reed, and turns to face the rest

John What were you doing behind the curtain?
Narrators I was reading.
John Show the book.
Narrators I fetched it.
John You have no business to take our books. You are a dependent. Mamma says you have no money. Your father left you none. You ought to beg. I'll teach you to rummage through my bookshelves — for they are mine. All the house belongs to me, or will do in a few years. Go and stand by the door, out of the way of the mirror and the windows.
First Narrator I did so ——
Second Narrator — not at first aware what was his intention.
Third Narrator But when I saw him lift and poise the book ——
Fourth Narrator — and stand in act to hurl it, I instinctively started aside——
Fifth Narrator — with a cry of alarm.
Sixth Narrator Not soon enough however—the volume was flung, it hit me and I fell ——
Narrators — striking my head against the door and cutting it.

Over which the Lights fade, the Narrators rush off and Jane is thrust on to the stage by Bessie, the nurse, and Miss Abbot, a lady's maid

The Lights come up on:

SCENE 1

The Red Room, Gateshead Hall

This may be represented by nothing more than a flowing deep red curtain

Jane (*kicking and fighting every inch of the way*) No. (*Pause*) No! No!
Bessie She's like a wild thing! She's like a mad cat!
Miss Abbot For shame! For shame! The devil's in her!
Jane But I have done nothing!
Bessie Nothing, miss? You struck the young gentleman.
Jane He struck me first! He struck me twice! He torments me! He is a bully and a coward.
Miss Abbot He is your benefactress's son. Your young master.

Jane Master! How is he my master? Am I a servant then?

Miss Abbot No — you are less than a servant, miss, for you do nothing for your keep. (*She pushes Jane down on to the floor*) There — stay there and dwell upon your wickedness.

Bessie If you won't stay still, you must be tied down. Miss Abbot, lend me your garters — she would break mine directly.

Miss Abbot is about to hoist her skirt up in order to remove her garter

Jane (*beseeching*) Don't tie me down. I promise not to stir.

Bessie She never did so before.

Miss Abbot But it was always in her, Bessie. I've told missis often about my opinion of the child, and missis agrees with me. She's an underhanded little thing.

Bessie You ought to know, Miss Eyre, that you are under obligation to Mrs Reed. She took you in when your parents died. If she were to turn you out, you would needs must go to the poorhouse.

Miss Abbot And you ought not to think yourself equal with the Misses and Master Reed. It is your place to be humble.

Bessie It's true, Miss Eyre, and for your own good.

Miss Abbot God will strike her dead one of these fine days. You mark my words and then where will she go — straight to hell-fire, I have no doubt. We'll leave her here to think on that.

Jane No. No. Don't leave me! Not in the Red Room. Mr Reed died in here. It's haunted.

Miss Abbot You'll do well to say your prayers then, won't you, miss? For if you don't repent, something evil might be permitted down that chimney to fetch you away — or straight through that window on big, black wings, perhaps. Come, Bessie.

Bessie and Miss Abbot exit

Jane Don't leave me alone! No! Don't leave me alone ...

But Bessie and Miss Abbot are already gone. There is the sound of the wind again as the Lights fade and come up instantly, on:

SCENE 2

The Drawing Room, Gateshead Hall

Mrs Reed and Mr Brocklehurst, a tall, harsh, prim man, enter in conversation. Mr Brocklehurst is carrying a book

Mrs Reed As I intimated in my letter, Mr Brocklehurst, the girl has neither the character nor the disposition I would wish. Should you admit her into Lowood School, I would be glad if the superintendent and teachers were requested to keep a strict eye on her.

Jane enters nervously

I was just telling Mr Brocklehurst, Jane, to instruct his staff to guard against your worst fault: a tendency to deceit. And I mention it too, in your hearing, that you may not attempt to impose on him or them.

Brocklehurst Her size is small. What is her age?

Mrs Reed Ten years.

Brocklehurst So much? (*He beckons Jane towards him with crooked forefinger*) Your name, little girl?

Jane Jane Eyre, sir.

Brocklehurst No sight so sad as that of a naughty child. Do you know where the wicked go after death?

Jane They go to hell.

Brocklehurst And what is hell, can you tell me that?

Jane A pit full of fire.

Brocklehurst And what must you do to avoid it?

Jane I must keep in good health and not die.

Brocklehurst How can you keep in good health? Children younger than you die daily. I buried a little child of five years old only a day or two since — a good little child, whose soul is now in heaven. It is feared that the same could not be said of you, were you to be summoned thence. (*To Mrs Reed*) Deceit is a sad fault in a child — a deceitful child is the next thing to an outright liar. She shall be watched, Mrs Reed. I will speak to Miss Temple and the teachers.

Mrs Reed I should wish her to be brought up in a manner suiting her prospects: to be useful, to be kept humble. As for the vacations, she will, with your permission, spend them always at the school.

Brocklehurst Your decisions are perfectly judicious, madam. Humility is a Christian grace. Little girl, here is a book entitled *The Child's Guide*.

He gives the book to Jane

Read it with prayer, especially that part containing "an account of the awfully sudden death of Martha Grantham, a naughty child addicted to falsehood". (*To Mrs Reed*) And now I must bid you good-morning.

Brocklehurst exits

Mrs Reed (*turning on Jane; angrily*) Go out of the room. Return to the nursery.

Jane I am not deceitful. If I were, I should say that I loved you, Aunt Reed. But I declare that I do not love you. I dislike you the worst of anybody in the world. And this book about the Liar, you may give it to your daughter, Georgina, for it is she who tells lies and not I!

Jane throws the book down on the floor at Mrs Reed's feet and storms out of the room as the Lights fade and come up immediately on two of the Narrators, standing at either end of the gallery

First Narrator Five o'clock had hardly struck on the morning of the nineteenth of January. I was already up and nearly dressed.

Second Narrator I was to leave Gateshead that day by coach which passed the lodge at six a.m.

First Narrator Bessie was the only person yet risen.

By which time, the Lights have come up on:

SCENE 3

The Driveway, Gateshead Hall

It is a chill winter's morning before first light and we can hear the sound of impatient horses anxious to be off. The Groom puts down a lantern. Bessie hands him a small trunk and he takes it off to load on to the coach

Bessie picks up the lantern which the Groom has put down as Jane enters

Bessie Did you go in and bid Mrs Reed goodbye?

Jane Your missis, Bessie, has not been my friend — she has been my foe.

Bessie Don't say that, Miss Jane.

Jane What does it matter? I shall soon have another set of people to dread.
Bessie If you dread them, they'll dislike you.
Jane As you do, Bessie?
Bessie I don't dislike you, miss. Why, I am fonder of you than of the other children.
Jane You've never shown it.
Bessie And you're so glad to leave me?
Jane Not at all, Bessie. Just now I am rather sorry.
Bessie I dare say now if I were to ask you for a goodbye kiss, you wouldn't give it to me?
Jane I'll kiss you goodbye and welcome, Bessie.

They embrace, warmly

   The Groom returns and gently prises Jane loose

Groom The coach is waiting. Come on, Miss Eyre.
Jane Goodbye to Gateshead Hall.

   Jane exits to join the coach

 Bessie and the Groom watch her go

Groom How far is it?
Bessie Fifty miles.
Groom What a long way! I wonder Mrs Reed is not afraid to trust her so far alone.
Bessie She's a strange child. A lonely frightened little thing. (*She calls to the coach driver*) Be sure and take good care of her!

As we hear the coach rattle off along the drive, the Groom puts an arm around Bessie's waist which surprises but does not displease her. The Lights fade on the Driveway and come up on the gallery

First Narrator I remember but little of the journey here to Lowood Orphanage — except that we travelled from before first light until very late last night. Yesterday the fear of the unknown drove away my appetite.
Second Narrator This morning I was ravenous except the porridge that

was given to us for breakfast was so burnt that not a single girl that I saw managed more than a spoonful — even a teacher said that it was "abominable stuff" and "shameful".

Over which, the Lights have come up on:

SCENE 4

A Classroom, Lowood School

Some half-dozen Girl Orphans (Jane is one of them) are standing behind child-size chairs. There is also a blackboard. Miss Temple, the school superintendent, aged thirty, wearing a "purple dress trimmed with black velvet and with a gold watch at her girdle" is in conversation with Mr Brocklehurst

Miss Temple   I must be responsible for the circumstance, sir. The breakfast was so ill-prepared that the pupils could not possibly eat it. And I dare not let them remain fasting until dinner time.

Brocklehurst's reply is intended for the pupils as well as Miss Temple and he prowls around the class as he delivers it

Brocklehurst   Madam, allow me an instant. You are aware that my plan in bringing up these girls is not to accustom them to habits of luxury and indulgence, but to render them hardy, patient, self-denying. Should any little accidental disappointment of the appetite occur, a brief address on those occasions would not be mistimed, wherein a judicious instructor would take the opportunity of referring to the sufferings of the primitive Christians; to the torments of martyrs; to the exhortations of Our Blessed Lord Himself, calling upon his disciples to take up their cross and follow Him; to His warnings that man shall not live by bread alone, but by every word that proceedeth out of the mouth of God; to His divine consolations, "If ye suffer hunger or thirst for My sake, happy are ye." Oh, madam, when you put bread and cheese, instead of burnt porridge, into these children's mouths, you may indeed feed their vile bodies — but you little think how you starve their immortal soul! Have them all sit down — except Helen Burns.
Miss Temple   Sit down, girls.

They all sit—with the exception of a frail girl, Helen Burns. Helen's cough has drawn Brocklehurst's attention to her

Brocklehurst (*prowling the classroom*) Straighten up, Burns. Burns, you poke your chin out most unpleasantly. Draw it in. Burns, I insist on you holding up your head, you dirty, disagreeable girl.

Unintentionally, Jane drops her slate which crashes on the floor. Brocklehurst speaks without looking round

A careless girl. It is the new pupil I perceive. I must not forget I have a word to say respecting her. Let the child who dropped her slate come forward.

As Jane crosses to the front of the class, Brocklehurst picks up the chair and places it for her to stand on. She does so

Miss Temple, children — you all see this girl? You observe that God has graciously given her the shape that he has given to all of us — who would think that the Evil One had already found a servant and an agent in her? It is my duty to warn you of this girl. Be on your guard against her. Shun her example. Avoid her company. Exclude her from your games. Shut her out of your conversations. Miss Temple, you will advise the staff to watch her carefully — to scrutinize her actions — to punish her body to save her soul — if, indeed, such salvation be possible. For this girl, this child, the native of a Christian land, worse than many a little heathen who says its prayers to Brahma and kneels before Juggernaut— this girl is — a liar! She has been sent here by her benefactress to be healed, even as the Jews of old sent their diseased to the troubled pool of ——

Brocklehurst now pauses intimidatingly at an Orphan's side, inviting her to nominate the location— luckily, she is able to do so

Orphan (*nervously*) Bethesda.

Brocklehurst (*patting the Orphan on the head*) Bethesda — I beg of all of you, do not allow the waters to stagnate around her. (*To Miss Temple*) Let her stand half an hour longer on that chair — and let no-one speak to her during the remainder of the day. Good-morning, girls.

Girls Good-morning, Mr Brocklehurst.

Brocklehurst indicates that he wishes to speak in private to Miss Temple, and then moves to leave

Miss Temple Class monitors — you will see to it that there is no talking until the bell rings for prayers. You will then proceed, in single file, and join the rest of the school in the assembly hall.

Helen raises her hand

Yes, Helen?
Helen Should I collect the slates, Miss Temple?
Miss Temple You may.

Miss Temple follows Mr Brocklehurst out of the room

Helen collects in the slates and, as she passes Jane, she manages to give her a brief smile

As a handbell rings somewhere in the school, the Girls file out of the room. Helen, bringing up the rear, pauses long enough to smile again at Jane

Jane, who has stood with bowed head throughout her time in front of the class, is uplifted

Jane (*to the audience*) How much strength did I draw from that smile! How much friendship glowed in her eyes. It was as if a martyr, a hero, I had read about in books, had passed a slave or a prisoner and given out strength in passing. I was not alone any longer! I was suddenly borne up!

The Light fades, temporarily, on Jane, and comes up on the Narrators about the stage

First Narrator 'Ere the half-hour ended as five o'clock struck——
Second Narrator — It was deep dusk and I retired into a corner and sank down on the floor ——
Third Narrator — overwhelmed with grief that seized me I sank with

my face to the ground—

Fourth Narrator — here I lay crushed and trodden on — could I ever rise more?

Fifth Narrator Never! I thought how ardently I wished to die ——

Sixth Narrator — whilst sobbing, someone approached me. Helen Burns was near.

The Lights come up on Jane who is huddled, sobbing, on the floor. Helen approaches her

Jane Helen, why do you stay with a girl whom everyone believes to be a liar? I know they despise me.

Helen Jane, you're mistaken. Probably not one in the school either despises or dislikes you.

Jane But if others don't love me, I'd rather die than live. I cannot bear to be solitary and hated, Helen. To gain some real affection from you or Miss Temple I would willingly submit to have the bone of my arm broken. Or to stand behind a kicking horse and let it dash its hoof at my chest.

Helen Hush, Jane.

Miss Temple enters

Miss Temple I came on purpose to find you, Miss Eyre. I want you in my room and as Helen Burns is with you, she may come too.

First Narrator We went. Following her guidance ——

Second Narrator — threading through intricate passages and mounting a staircase before we reached her apartment.

Jane and Helen move into the following scene, Miss Temple's apartment

The Lights fade and now come up on:

SCENE 5

Miss Temple's Apartment

Miss Temple's apartment is represented by three chairs and a side-table which is laid with tea and bread and butter for one. Miss Temple tugs an imaginary bell-rope

Miss Temple Is it all over? Have you cried your grief away?
Jane I am afraid that I shall never do that entirely.
Miss Temple Why?
Jane Because I have been wrongly accused --- and you, ma'am, and
  everybody else will think me wicked.
Miss Temple We shall think you what you prove yourself to be, my child.
  If you obey the rules and continue to behave yourself, you will satisfy
  us.
Jane Shall I, Miss Temple?
Miss Temple You will.

  A maid, Barbara, enters

  Barbara , I am just about to have tea and have two visitors. Would you
  bring me extra cups and a little more bread and butter? There is not
  enough for three.

  Barbara goes out

  Be seated, girls.

They sit

  How are you tonight, Helen? Have you coughed much today?
Helen Not quite so much, I think, ma'am.
Miss Temple And the pain in your chest?
Helen It is a little better.

Miss Temple crosses and takes Helen's pulse

Miss Temple You're both my guests tonight.

  *Barbara returns with a tray which holds two cups and saucers, which
  she places with the other tea-things*

  Where's the extra bread and butter?
Barbara Miss Temple, Mrs Harden says that she has already sent up the
  usual quantity.

Miss Temple Oh, very well. We must make it do, I suppose.

Barbara goes out

Fortunately, I have it in my power to supply deficiencies for this once.
(*She takes a small package out of a drawer in the table and unwraps it*)
I meant to give you both some of this fine seed-cake to take with you,
but as there is so little bread and butter, you must have it now.

*As Miss Temple serves the tea, the Lights fade on the scene and come up
on another area of stage where an orphan Girl holds a candle as she sings,
with piano accompaniment*

Girl   My feet they are sore, and my limbs they are weary,
                      Long is the way, and the mountains are wild;
                      Soon will the twilight close moonless and dreary
                      Over the path of the poor orphan child.

*The Girl has been joined by the other Orphans also carrying candles, and
they move forward, slowly, downstage, as they continue the song. During
the following a small iron-bound bed, covered with rough blankets, is set
behind the Girls*

Girls   Why did they send me so far and so lonely,
                      Up where the moors spread and grey rocks are pil'd?
                      Men are hard-hearted, and kind angels only
                      Watch o'er the steps of the poor orphan child.

                      Yet distant and soft, the night breeze is blowing,
                      Clouds there are none, and clear stars beam mild;
                      God, in his mercy, protection is showing,
                      Comfort and hope to the poor orphan child.

*As the song continues, Helen Burns, now wearing a night-gown, enters
from the rear and gets into the bed*

                      E'en should I fall by the broken bridge passing,
                      Or stray in the marshes, by false hopes beguil'd,
                      Still will my Father, with promise and blessing,
                      Take to his bosom the poor orphan child.

Scene 6

The Sick Room, Lowood School

The Girls blow out their candles and exit

A Nurse is sitting in a chair at the end of Helen's bed and is asleep. It is night, and there is one flickering candle on the floor. Jane tiptoes into the sick room

Jane Helen? Are you awake? Helen?

Helen (*close to death*) Can it be you, Jane? Why are you come here? It's past eleven o'clock — I heard the church clock strike some minutes since.

Jane They told me you were very ill. I couldn't sleep until I'd spoken to you.

Helen You came to say goodbye then? You are probably just in time.

Jane Are you going somewhere, Helen? Are you going home?

Helen coughs

Helen Yes. To my long home — my last home.

Jane No, no, Helen ...

Helen props herself up in bed

Helen I am very happy, Jane — and you must promise not to grieve for me when I am dead. There is nothing to grieve about. We must all die one day. My mind is at rest. I have no pain now. I am ready to go.

Jane But where are you going to, Helen? Do you know?

Helen I believe. I have faith, I am going to God.

Jane Where is God? What is God?

Helen He is our Maker, Jane, mine and yours. I believe both in His power and in His goodness.

Jane You are sure then, Helen, that there is such a place as heaven?

Helen I am sure that there is a future state and I count the hours until I am summoned there to meet Him face to face. He is my Father. He is my friend. I love Him and I believe that He loves me. How comfortable I am! But that last fit of coughing has tired me a little. Don't leave me,

Jane. I like to have you near me.
Jane I am here, dear Helen. No-one shall take me away.
Helen Jane, your little feet are bare. Lie down and cover yourself with my
    quilt.

Jane gets into the bed

Are you warm, darling?
Jane Yes, Helen.
Helen Good-night, Jane.
Jane Good-night, Helen.

*They sleep. The Lights fade down and up into morning. The Nurse wakes,
blows out her candle and crosses to the bed. Helen is dead, one arm hangs
lifeless. The Nurse gently wakens Jane*

Nurse Miss Eyre. Wake up, Miss Eyre.
Jane Helen, wake up. Helen. Helen, don't leave me. Helen, come back!
Nurse Come on, miss. (*She gently helps Jane to her feet and moves her
    some paces from the bed*) Stay there.

*The Nurse folds Helen's arms across her chest and then covers her face
with the blanket. Jane moves downstage to face the audience and sings.
While she is singing, the girls enter, solemnly, each one carrying a single
lily and the bed is struck*

Jane (*singing*)   There is thought that for strength should avail me;
                         Though both of shelter and kindred despoiled;
                         Heaven is a home, and rest will not fail me;
                         God is a friend to the poor orphan child.

*The Light fades up to day, the single tolling of a funeral bell changes into
a happy pealing, as we go to:*
                                   Scene 7

Outside St Stephen's Church, Lowood

Eight years later

Where tragedy is turned into joy as Miss Temple enters on the arm of her new husband, Mr Naysmith. The Girls' single lilies are collected together to become Miss Temple's bouquet. As the Girls chatter excitedly upstage with Mr Naysmith, Miss Temple moves downstage to meet Jane. Eight years have passed

Miss Temple Your kind thoughts, dearest Jane, mean more to me than those of any other person.

Jane They are heartfelt, Miss Temple — forgive me, Mrs Naysmith — of that, I promise you.

Miss Temple And what of you? Have you decided yet what's next, now that you are a woman? You could stay on at Lowood and continue teaching?

Jane Teaching, yes — but not at Lowood. Without you there, there is no place for me.

Miss Temple Then where? And how do you intend to find a position?

Jane I shall advertise.

Miss Temple Advertise?

Jane For a post as a private tutor: English, French, Drawing, Music — and in the *Yorkshire Herald*, where I have seen several such situations both advertised and sought for. You enclose the advertisement and the money to pay for it under a cover directed to the editor — I shall ask for answers, should there be any, to be addressed to me — I shall use my initials, J.E. — at the Post Office here in Lowood. Then, assuming that...

Having been carried away by her own enthusiasm, Jane realizes that the bridegroom Mr Naysmith, has approached and is holding out his hands to his bride, Jane kisses Miss Temple, impulsively

God bless you both and keep you very happy.

As the bride and groom go off, hand in hand, the Lights fade on the wedding scene and a spot comes up on Mrs Fairfax, an elderly lady in "widow's cap, black silk gown and snowy white muslin apron," who is standing on the gallery, reading a letter she has just penned

Mrs Fairfax If "J. E." who advertised in the *Yorkshire Herald* of last Thursday, possesses the acquirements mentioned — and if she is in a position to give satisfactory references as to character and competency——

Over which, the Lights come up on:

SCENE 8

Jane's Bedroom, Lowood School

Where Jane is kneeling on the floor, packing her trunk, as Mrs Fairfax continues

Mrs Fairfax ... situation can be offered here where there is but one pupil, a little girl, under ten years of age, and where the salary is thirty pounds per annum. J.E is requested to send references, name and address, and all particulars to the direction of Mrs Fairfax, Thornfield, near Millcote, West Yorkshire...

As the Light fades on Mrs Fairfax, a Porter enters Jane's room

Porter There is someone called to see you, Miss Eyre.
Jane To see me? You're mistaken, surely?

Bessie enters

Bessie No, Miss Jane, there is no mistake.

She nods to the Porter who goes out

You've not forgotten me, I think?
Jane Bessie! But you are fortunate to have found me — one day later, Bessie, and I would have been gone from this place.
Bessie I knew that, miss, from the letter you wrote to Mrs Reed.
Jane Only because she is my legal guardian still, and I needed her permission to leave — but otherwise I have neither set eyes on her nor made contact with her these past eight years. You are at Gateshead Hall still?

Overcome at this reunion after all the years, Jane hugs Bessie

Bessie! Bessie!

Bessie I am married now to Robert, the groom whom you may remember? And we have two children, Bobby and Jane. When I heard missis say you were going to another part of the country, I thought I'd just set off and get a look at you, before you were quite out of my reach. You're not grown so very tall, Miss Jane, nor so very stout. I dare say they've not kept you too well at this place — but here you are — a teacher now — and a room all to yourself.

Jane Half a room Bessie. There is a Miss Gryce who takes History and Geography and Bible Studies and snores. But I shall have a room of my own at Thornfield Hall.

Jane feels that Bessie is looking at her with a critical eye

Oh, I am afraid you are disappointed in me, Bessie?

Bessie No, Miss Jane, not exactly. You are genteel enough. You look like a lady — and it is as much as I ever expected of you. You were no beauty as a child. I daresay you are clever though. You play the piano?

Jane A little.

Bessie And can draw and paint?

Jane Yes.

Bessie And you have learnt French?

Jane Yes, Bessie, I can both read it and speak it.

Bessie Oh, you are quite a lady, Miss Jane! You will get on whether your relations notice you or not — which brings me to another matter: have you heard anything from your father's kinsfolk, the Eyres? Missis said that they were poor and not worth speaking to — only one day, several months ago this was, a Mr Eyre came to the house and asked to see you. Mrs Reed told him you was away at school. He was that disappointed. He was sailing off to a foreign land the very next day and so could not arrange to see you. But I managed to pass a word with him and he gave me this to pass on to you. (*She produces a scrap of paper which she hands to Jane*) He said he was your father's brother — his address I believe it is. He said he would dearly like to hear from you.

Jane And I from him, Bessie.

Bessie Missis would scarcely give him the time of day — you know how short she can be with them she takes against.

Jane As well as anyone knows, Bessie.

The Porter returns

Jane nods at him

He carries out the trunk

But let's not dwell on Mrs Reed. We have such little time to spend together, I would rather talk of more pleasant matters. (*She puts on her bonnet, gloves and shawl*) Come, let us go out into the grounds until the carriage is ready and you shall tell me all about your children.
Bessie And I'm anxious to hear your news, Miss Jane. Missis let out that you'd secured a post as a governess?

Jane and Bessie move downstage as the Lights come up on:

Scene 9

Thornfield Hall

Adele Varens, a pretty girl, about eight years old, whose waist-length hair and expensive Parisian clothes are in sharp contrast to the plain dresses of the orphan girls at Lowood School, is sitting on the floor, turning the pages of a book, as Jane continues talking to Bessie, downstage

Jane To a family by the name of Fairfax, Bessie, that live at a Thornfield Hall, near Millcote, and with just one child that I shall have charge of — though what kind of folk they are, or what manner of place it is, or even what future lies in store for me, I know not — except that I hope with all my heart that my time at Thornfield may serve to provide me with happier memories than many of those I shall take with me from Lowood.

As Jane and Bessie move off, there is the sound of low, mocking laughter from an upstairs room at Thornfield

Adele, immersed in her book, does not seem to have noticed

Leah, a housemaid in her late teens, appears on the gallery, slightly flustered as if the laughter may have caused her some concern

Leah Miss Adele? Are you downstairs or up?
Adele (*to herself; studying a picture in her book*) *La Belle et La Bête.*
  Voici la Belle! Voici la Bête!

Leah arrives downstairs and discovers Adele

Leah There you are! You've had me at my wit's end, lass! Your nursery
  tea's going begging on the table, clap cold I shouldn't wonder.

*Adele, who does not appear to speak a word of English, gazes at Leah
puzzled but makes no move. Leah, vexed, takes the book from out of
Adele's hands and uses it as "bait" to tempt her from the room*

  Adele scurries off

Leah remains behind

  John, a manservant, carries in Jane's trunk

Leah That can stop where it is for now.

John puts down the trunk

  Jane enters

Jane I am Jane Eyre.
Leah Shall you come in, ma'am? I'll mix you some hot water and wine
  and fetch you sandwiches. Mrs Fairfax will be here directly.

  John exits followed by Leah

Jane is alone and looking hesitantly around

  Mrs Fairfax enters

Mrs Fairfax How do you do, Miss Eyre. I'm Mrs Fairfax.
Jane I'm pleased to meet you.
Mrs Fairfax Take off your things and come over by the fire. You must
  be frozen after all that time in the coach. I'm glad to have you here —

it will be much more pleasant having a companion in the house.

Jane (*taking off her bonnet and shawl*) Shall I have the pleasure of seeing Miss Fairfax tonight?

Mrs Fairfax Miss Fairfax? Oh, you mean Miss Varens! Your pupil's name is Varens. Adele Varens. She is not related to me — I have no family, Miss Eyre, which is why Thornfield Hall has been a lonely place, except for the servants. It's a pleasing home, but I'm afraid it will be getting out of order, unless Mr Rochester should take it into his head to come and live here permanently.

Jane Mr Rochester? Who is he?

Mrs Fairfax Why, the owner of Thornfield.

Jane I thought Thornfield belonged to you?

Mrs Fairfax To me? Bless you, child, what an idea! I am only the housekeeper. Adele is Mr Rochester's ward. She's French — and speaks very little English, which is partly why I was requested to find a governess for her.

Jane What kind of a man is Mr Rochester?

Mrs Fairfax One that has travelled widely — he has a gentleman's tastes and habits and expects things to be done the way he likes them.

Jane Is he himself a likeable man?

Mrs Fairfax His tenants will tell you that he's a fair and liberal landlord, although he has not spent much time amongst them.

Jane Do you like him?

Mrs Fairfax I have never had much conversation with him — I dare say he is clever, but he's a strange man to get to know.

Jane In what way is he strange?

Mrs Fairfax You must wait and judge for yourself.

Leah enters with Jane's supper tray

Here's Leah with some supper for you. Leah, perhaps Miss Eyre would rather you took it up to her room — she's been travelling since early morning. There's been a fire lit for several hours and I will arrange to have your trunk sent up to you — if you are at all like me, you won't feel completely settled until you've unpacked your things.

Jane Thank you, Leah, I would like to see my room.

Leah goes out with the tray

Mrs Fairfax Miss Eyre, when you do meet Mr Rochester, whether or not
you understand him will be of little consequence. He is a very good
master.

*As Jane crosses to follow Leah, we hear again the unearthly laughter from
somewhere upstairs. Jane, startled, turns back to Mrs Fairfax*

Jane What was that?
Mrs Fairfax Some of the servants, very likely. Perhaps Grace Poole. She
sews in one of the upstairs rooms. (*She calls upstairs*) Grace! (*To Jane*)
She is someone who helps Leah with the housework.

*Grace Poole, a "woman of between thirty and forty: a set square-made
figure with a hard, plain face", appears on the gallery*

Too much noise, Grace. Remember the rules.

Grace inclines her head and goes without a word

She is not the most forthcoming of servants, but she does all that is
required of her. But Leah will be waiting for you — good-night, Miss
Eyre.
Jane Good-night, Mrs Fairfax.

*As Jane moves to exit, the Lights fade and we hear again the soughing of
the moorland wind. The Lights come up slowly on:*

SCENE 10

A Country Lane

*As the howling wind continues, accompanied now by lightning and the
sound of thunder, we hear the sound of approaching hoofbeats and then a
sudden whinny. Mr Rochester hurtles on to the stage, full-length, as the
wind dies and there is moonlight. Jane hurries to where Mr Rochester is
feeling at his leg. He is a dark-faced, stern-featured, heavily built man in
his late thirties*

Jane Are you hurt, sir? If you need help I can fetch someone from either

Thornfield Hall or from Hay.

Rochester Thank you, but there are no bones broken — I shall manage well enough.

Jane I can hardly leave you, sir, at so late an hour, in this empty lane, with your horse bolted and when you plainly cannot walk.

Rochester (*giving Jane his full attention for the first time*) I should think you ought to be at home yourself, if you have a home in the neighbourhood. Where do you come from?

Jane From just below and I'm not afraid of being out at night when there's a moon to guide me.

Rochester You live just below, you say? Do you mean at that house with the battlements?

Jane Yes, sir.

Rochester Whose house is it?

Jane Mr Rochester's.

Rochester Do you know Mr Rochester?

Jane I have not met him, no.

Rochester He's not resident then?

Jane No.

Rochester Do you know where he is?

Jane I don't. I will run over to Hay for you, with pleasure, if it will help you. Indeed, I am on my way there now to post a letter.

Rochester You're not a servant at the house, are you?

Jane I'm the governess.

Rochester The governess, are you?

Jane I am Jane Eyre.

Rochester Well then, Jane Eyre — I can't commission you to fetch help, but you may help me a little yourself, if you will be so kind.

Jane Yes, sir.

Rochester beckons Jane towards him and she helps him to his feet

Rochester Necessity compels me to make you useful. My horse, if I'm not mistaken, has gone no further than that quarry. If you'll help me hobble close to him, I can get back into the saddle.

Jane I am pleased to do anything, sir, that will be of help.

Jane, supporting Rochester, assists him to hobble off stage

The Lights fade

SCENE 11

Thornfield Hall

It is night and Leah comes down the stairs, carrying a candle in one hand to light her way, and an empty water-jug and soiled towel in the other, as Mrs Fairfax enters, briskly

Mrs Fairfax Kitty! Leah! John!

There is as much to and fro'ing of servants as can be mustered, with warming pans, bed linen, etc., being transported towards the stairs. During which, chairs, footstools, a small table, etc., are set to represent the drawing-room. To add to the general confusion, a dog is barking continuously

Jane enters the scene

Jane (*entering*) Whose is the dog that's fastened in the yard?
Mrs Fairfax The master's back.
Jane Mr Rochester?
Mrs Fairfax And he's had an accident.
Jane Mr Rochester?
Mrs Fairfax His horse slipped on ice — the surgeon's with him —it's always treacherous up on that hill at this time of year. Thank heaven it's nothing serious; a bad sprain at the most. But it's put us all at sixes and sevens. Will he want his dinner in the dining-room or take supper in his bedchamber? I can't go and interrupt to ask while Mr Carter's with him. And that's another problem: will he be eating alone, or inviting the surgeon to take a bite with him? And will someone do something to stop that dog from barking?

As if on cue, the dog stops barking

Leah enters, carrying a tray on which is a brandy decanter and two glasses

I'll take that up, Leah, if you will light the way — at least it will give me cause to go into his chamber.

Leah gives her the tray and takes up a candelabra

We do know something of his intentions for tomorrow — he's said that he'd be glad if you and your pupil would take tea with him.
Jane Of course. How long will Mr Rochester be staying, Mrs Fairfax?
Mrs Fairfax That's a question none can answer save Mr Rochester.

As Mrs Fairfax leaves and Jane takes off her shawl and bonnet, the Lights fade, momentarily, and come up again on the same scene, a day later, lit by several candles

Mr Rochester is sitting on a chair, resting his leg on a footstool. Mrs Fairfax is sitting on a second chair, pouring tea at a side-table. Adele is sitting on the floor, playing with a new doll

Jane enters the scene

Mrs Fairfax Here is Miss Eyre, sir.
Rochester (*without so much as a glance*) Let Miss Eyre be seated.
Adele Voilà, Mademoiselle Eyre! Voici mon cadeau!
Jane C'est jolie, Adele.
Mrs Fairfax Will you hand Mr Rochester's cup?

Jane passes the cup of tea to Rochester. He holds her enquiring glance for a moment, but makes no reference to their previous day's encounter nor does he give any sign of recognizing her

Adele N'est-ce pas, monsieur, qu'il y a un cadeau pour Mademoiselle Eyre dans votre coffre?
Rochester Did you expect a present, Miss Eyre? Are you fond of presents?
Jane I hardly know, sir. I have little experience of them — they are generally thought pleasant things.
Rochester Generally thought? But what do you think?
Jane I should need to give time to such a question, sir, before venturing an answer. A present can be given for all kinds of reasons — and those reasons being as important as the gift itself.

Rochester You are not as unsophisticated as Adele, Miss Eyre. She always demands a "cadeau" the moment I set foot in the house. You're more inclined to beat about the bush.

Jane But with good cause. Adele and yourself are old acquaintances. You are in the habit of giving her playthings. I am a stranger, sir, and have done nothing to deserve a present.

Rochester Oh come, Miss Eyre — false modesty doesn't suit you at all! I have been talking to the child. I am amazed at how much she has improved under your tutelage.

Jane Thank you, sir. You have given me my present — it is the one which all teachers crave: praise of their pupil's progress.

Rochester Where were you before you came to Thornfield?

Jane At Lowood School in Derbyshire.

Rochester Isn't that a charitable concern? And how long were you there?

Jane Eight years.

Rochester Eight years! You must have an inner strength, Miss Eyre! I would have sworn that half that length of time in such an institution would have broken the spirit of a full grown man — let alone a frail thing such as yourself. No wonder you have the look of another world. I marvelled where you got that sort of face — and I'm not decided yet. Who are your parents?

Jane I have none.

Rochester Do you remember them?

Jane No.

Rochester Well then, if you disown parents, you must have some sort of kinsfolk. Uncles? Aunts?

Jane None that I ever saw.

Rochester And your home?

Jane I have no home either.

Rochester Who recommended you to come here?

Jane I advertised — and Mrs Fairfax answered my advertisement.

Mrs Fairfax And I give thanks to Providence every day for guiding me in the decision. Miss Eyre has not only proved a kind and careful teacher to Adele, she has also been a caring companion for myself.

Rochester There is no need to give her a character, Mrs Fairfax — I am capable of making up my own mind. What age were you when you went to Lowood?

Jane Ten years and three months.

Rochester And you stayed there for eight years. Then you are eighteen now?

Jane I am.

Rochester Arithmetic, you see, is useful — without its aid I should not have known your age, for I could never have guessed at it by looking at you. And what did you learn at Lowood? Can you play the piano?

Jane A little.

Rochester An answer that might mean anything or nothing. Play something for me now. (*Less brusquely*) If it would please you.

Jane picks up a candle and crosses to the piano. She plays the "Poor Orphan Child" theme. The tranquillity of the scene is broken by the sound of the mocking laughter. Jane does not hear it but Rochester's mood darkens. He gets to his feet, raises his stick and brings it crashing down on the arm of his chair

Rochester It is getting late. It is time Adele returned to the nursery, Miss Eyre. And I have business to attend to. I bid you all good-night.

Jane *Ici, Adele.*

Adele scampers out and Rochester goes off in a different direction

Jane You spoke truthfully, Mrs Fairfax, when you said that he was a strange man to know.

Mrs Fairfax I am used to him — and if, at times, he may seen strange, Miss Eyre, one must be prepared to make allowances.

Jane Why?

Mrs Fairfax Partly because it is his nature — and partly because there are private, painful matters that trouble him.

The Lights fade and come up on four Narrators on the gallery

First Narrator For several subsequent days I saw little of Mr Rochester.

Second Narrator In the mornings he seemed much engaged with business.

Third Narrator In the afternoon, gentlemen from Millcote or the neighbourhood called and sometimes stayed to dine.

Fourth Narrator After his sprain was well enough to admit of horse exercise, he rode out a great deal, probably to return those visits.

The Light fades on the Narrators and comes up on:

Scene 12

The Garden, Thornfield Hall

Where Jane is sitting on a travel rug. There is an open portfolio of watercolour paintings and pencil drawings at her side. She is at work on a new pencil sketch and does not notice Rochester as he approaches and looks over her shoulder

Rochester I perceive, Miss Eyre, that you do not draw from nature?
Jane (*startled*) Out of my head.
Rochester The same head that is on your shoulders?
Jane Yes, sir.
Rochester Has it other furniture of the same kind within?
Jane I should think it may have. Better, I should hope.

Rochester picks up several of the paintings. All of Jane's work has been wrested from her imagination and is dreamlike in conception — for a detailed description of the portfolio's contents, refer to the novel, Chapter 13. Rochester leafs through the pictures

Rochester You've given much time and thought to these. When did you do them?
Jane During my last year at Lowood — in the vacations. When I had nothing else to occupy me.
Rochester Were you happy when you painted them?
Jane I was absorbed — yes, I was happy. Painting them provided me with one of the keenest pleasures I have ever known.

While Rochester is studying the paintings Jane studies him

Rochester That's not saying much — your pleasures, by your own account, have not been many — but I dare say it took you into a kind of artist's dreamland. These eyes that you have given to the Evening Star, they could only have come from a dream. And who taught you to paint wind? (*He realizes that Jane has been studying him*) You examine me, Miss Eyre — do you find me handsome?
Jane No, sir.

Rochester By my word, but there is something most decidedly singular about you! I've watched you, often, sitting, keeping silent — but when someone does force you into saying something — you rap out an answer which, if not blunt, is certainly to the point. Go on then, if you don't like my looks, tell me what's wrong with them? You'll grant me, at least, that I have all my limbs and features like any other man? Supposing I were to play you at your own game, Miss Eyre, and tell you that you are not pretty any more than I am handsome?

Jane does not reply

It's back to silence, is it? I don't want your silences, young lady, not this afternoon. This afternoon I am in a mood for conversation. It would please me to learn more about you. Speak.

Jane What about, sir?

Rochester Whatever you like. I leave both the choice of subject and the manner of treating it entirely to yourself.

Again he waits for her to reply but she is silent

You are dumb, Miss Eyre? Stubborn?

Jane I am more than willing to talk to you, sir — but don't ask me to introduce a topic. How am I to know what will interest you? You ask me the questions and I will do my best to answer them.

Rochester Very well — then tell me this: you've already said that you don't approve of my looks — do you also think me a fool?

Jane Far from it.

Rochester Or even a villain?

Jane No, sir — I have even heard you referred to as being both fair and just.

Rochester Whoever told you that, Miss Eyre, is a downright liar. Once perhaps ... When I was your age, yes, I had a tenderness of heart. But I have suffered too much since then. I have been knocked about by fortune. What fate has handed out to me has turned me into a desperate man — even degenerate. I wish I had stood firm against it. God knows I do! Whenever you are tempted to stray, Miss Eyre, shun remorse. Remorse is life's poison.

Jane Repentance is said to be its cure, sir.

Rochester Since happiness is denied me, I intend to get nothing but pleasure from life.

Jane Then you will degenerate still more, sir.

Rochester Perhaps — perhaps not. Why should I, if I can get sweet, fresh pleasure? And I may get it as sweet and as fresh as the wild honey the bee gathers on the moor.

Jane Then you will get stung. It will taste bitter, sir.

Rochester (*laughing*) How do you know? You have never tried it. You are not my conscience, young lady. Such a serious, such a solemn person! You could laugh as merrily as anyone — but in the presence of a man, Miss Eyre, you are afraid to smile too gaily, to speak too freely, to move too quickly. But in time — in time — I think you will be natural with me! Sometimes, you have the look of a small, wild bird peering out through the close-set bars of a cage — if someone could only set it free, it would soar cloud high ...

Jane has gathered her things together

Where are you going?

Jane The afternoon is gone, sir, and I have Adele to attend to.

Rochester Stay a moment longer. There is something else I wish to tell you. Do you ever wonder about the true identity of Adele Varens?

Jane That she is more than your ward, sir, she is your daughter?

Rochester (*shaking his head*) I loved her mother, yes — years ago. Celine Varens was a French opera dancer for whom I cherished a *grande passion*— until I called upon her unexpectedly one afternoon and found her entertaining another man. You never felt jealousy, did you, Miss Eyre? Of course not — because you have never felt love. Some years later she left him too and ran off to Italy with some sort of singer or musician, leaving behind the child of that relationship — not mine, though the woman tried to tell me that it was. But I took the poor thing out of the slime and mud of Paris and brought it here.

Jane Hardly the deed, sir, of a degenerate man?

Rochester But now that you know that your protégée is the illegitimate offspring of a French opera girl, you will perhaps think differently of your post? You will be coming to me soon with notice that you have found another place?

Jane No — if anything the opposite. Now that I know that she is parentless — deserted by her mother and disowned by you, sir, I shall hold her more dearly than before.

Rochester nods gravely

Rochester (*dismissing the subject*) I like this day. I like that sky of steel.
I even dare to like Thornfield — and yet for how long have I hated its
very name? And how much hatred is in my heart still for ... ?

*Leaving the sentence unfinished, he turns and walks off. Jane hesitates
then follows Rochester*

Once again, we hear the ripple of maniacal laughter. The Lights fade

*In the half-dark on the gallery, we do no more than glimpse the tall
figure of Bertha Mason, in a shapeless night-gown, her long tousled
black hair half-covering her face and carrying a rush torch which is
glowing red, laughing hysterically as she hastens in and out of view*

The Lights fade completely on the gallery and comes up immediately on:

Scene 13

Rochester's Bedroom

*This is represented by a long white muslin curtain upon which, reflected
from behind, we see the growing flickering tongues of flame. Jane crosses
to Rochester's bedroom*

Jane Who's there? (*She becomes aware of the growing fire, she rushes
across and rips down the curtain — smoke billows everywhere*) Wake!
Wake, sir! Rouse yourself!

*As Jane stamps out the fire, Rochester stumbles through the smoke,
fastening his dressing-gown*

Rochester What is it? Is that Jane Eyre?
Jane In heaven's name, get up, sir!

Mrs Fairfax enters

Mrs Fairfax What's happened, sir? Oh, God, Mr Rochester, how did this...

Rochester There is no harm done, Mrs Fairfax —except for the curtains.

Mrs Fairfax I shall attend to the matter, sir.

Mrs Fairfax exits

Rochester I would appreciate it if you would not discuss this matter with anyone — not even with Mrs Fairfax.

Jane If that is your wish, sir. Good-night then.

Rochester What! Are you leaving me already? Why, you have just this minute saved my life — and you walk away from me as if we were mutual strangers. At least shake my hand.

After a moment's hesitation, Jane proffers her hand and he grips it tightly

I knew, from the very moment I set eyes on you, that it was not mere chance that had directed you towards me. I knew it when I looked into your eyes — there was something deep inside them, Jane, that caught at my innermost heart. And now — I owe you my life. How can I ever repay you?

Jane I am only glad that I happened to be awake, sir. Good-night again.

Rochester What? You *will* go?

Jane I am cold, sir.

Rochester Cold? Yes—forgive me, it's a chilly night. Go then, Jane. Go! (*But he makes no sign of letting go of her hand*)

Jane I think I hear Mrs Fairfax returning, sir.

Rochester Leave me then.

And, at last, he does release his hold on her. Jane goes out, leaving him to contemplate the damaged curtain

Mrs Fairfax returns

Mrs Fairfax She somehow succeeded in escaping, sir, but is safely returned now and locked inside her room.

Rochester I only give thanks to God that there was not more serious damage done.

And, as they hold each other's concerned glance, the Lights fade and come up immediately on:

Scene 14

The Gallery

Grace Poole is holding a tray of food and is in conversation with Leah who is holding the damaged curtain

While they are speaking Jane arrives on the gallery accompanied by Adele

Grace It's a mercy master wasn't burnt alive in his bed!

Leah How did it happen? Has anybody said?

Grace He fell asleep, by all accounts, with the window open and a candle burning by his bed. A draught must have tugged at the bed-curtains.

Leah Good-morning, Miss Eyre.

Jane Good-morning, Leah.

Jane ushers Adele in the direction of the nursery as Leah moves off towards the kitchen

Mrs Poole?

Grace Yes, miss?

Jane Last night's accident — did Mr Rochester wake nobody? Did no-one hear him move?

Grace considers the question

Grace Not that I've heard of. The servants sleep so far off, miss, that they wouldn't have heard anything anyway. Mrs Fairfax's room and yours are nearest to the master's. Mrs Fairfax says she heard nothing. Did you hear any noise?

Jane Yes — I heard someone laughing.

Grace Laughing, miss? It would hardly likely to be the master, would it, miss? Not when he was in danger. Perhaps you dreamed it.

Jane It was no dream, Mrs Poole.

Grace No, miss? You didn't think to open the door and look out on the gallery?

Jane I did but there was no-one there.

Grace You might do better to keep it shut, miss, and bolted. We've never had any robbers in as yet — it's a quiet enough neighbourhood as any — but there's always a first time for everything — and there aren't that many servants kept here, with the master spending so much time away.

Mrs Fairfax returns

Yes, Mrs Fairfax?

Mrs Fairfax The servants' dinner will be ready soon — will you come down?

Grace (*indicating her tray*) I've got my pint of porter and a bit of pudding, Mrs Fairfax, I shan't want for more.

As Grace exits, Mrs Fairfax peers out over the gallery

During the following Jane and Mrs Fairfax are held in a spot

Mrs Fairfax Spring seems to be on its way at last. The weather's broken nicely in time for Mr Rochester's journey.

Jane Is Mr Rochester going away?

Mrs Fairfax He's gone already. He breakfasted in his room before dawn had broken and left with the early light.

Jane Do you expect him back tonight?

Mrs Fairfax No — nor tomorrow neither. It wouldn't come as any surprise if we didn't set eyes on him for a week or even more. He's gone over to visit Lord Ingram at Gorstone Hall which is always full of guests at this time of year — but I daresay it'll be Blanche Ingram, not the dancing, that'll keep the master dallying at Gorstone.

Jane Blanche Ingram?

Mrs Fairfax Lord Ingram's younger sister. An honourable. She set her cap at the master the very first time she ever came here — and she was no more then than a slip of a girl, all of seven years ago.

Jane Have you seen her, Mrs Fairfax? What is she like?

Mrs Fairfax Yes, I saw her. It was Christmas time and the house was all lit up and decorated. The servants were allowed into the hall to watch the dancing and to listen to the ladies sing and play. I never set eyes on anything as splendid in my entire life. All of the ladies were beautiful and beautifully dressed — but Miss Blanche, there's no denying that she was queen ...

With Jane and Mrs Fairfax still held in the spot, bring Lights up on:

SCENE 15

The Ballroom, Gorstone Hall

*This will be established by an attendant liveried Footman and a candle-
lit chandelier — under which light Rochester is waltzing with the twenty-
five-year-old Blanche Ingram, as Jane continues on the gallery*

Jane And will there be dancing, Mrs Fairfax, at Lord Ingram's home?
Mrs Fairfax There's sure to be. Most folk think they'd make the best
   match in the county.

The spotlight fades on the gallery

*Mrs Fairfax leaves the gallery while on the ballroom floor the waltz ends
and Blanche and Rochester move away as six of Lord Ingram's Guests
enter, in pairs — some of them sip at glasses of wine; some of the ladies
are fanning themselves, elegantly. The three pairs continue separate
conversations*

First Guest She is greatly admired, of course.
Second Guest Yes, indeed, not only for her beauty but for her accom-
   plishments.
Third Guest Wasn't she one of the ladies who sang earlier?
Fourth Guest Yes, a gentleman accompanied her. She and Mr Rochester
   sang a duet.
Fifth Guest Mr Rochester? I was not aware that he could sing?
Sixth Guest Oh, but he has a fine bass voice and an excellent taste for
   music.
First Guest And this beautiful accomplished lady, she is not yet married?
Second Guest It appears not. I fancy neither she nor her sister have very
   large fortunes.
Third Guest Old Lord Ingram's estates were chiefly entailed and the
   eldest son came in for almost everything.
Fourth Guest I wonder no wealthy nobleman or gentleman has taken a
   fancy to her.

Fifth Guest Mr Rochester, for instance, he is rich is he not?
Sixth Guest Oh, yes! But you see, there is a considerable difference in age.
First Guest Mr Rochester is nearly forty, she is but twenty-five.
Second Guest What of that? More unequal matches are made every day.

The Lights fade on the ballroom. Snap on spotlight on Jane alone on the gallery and gazing out into the audience

Jane Look at yourself, Jane Eyre — for shame! How did you see yourself before? Did you imagine, for one moment, that he was taken with you? Did you believe, for one single second, that there was something about you that might please him? Him? You! Whatever did you think you were? What did you imagine you were about? I'll tell you what you are going to do, lady. Now, beginning this instant — you will take up your chalks and sketching paper; you will look into this mirror which has no secrets — and you will draw your face, as it is, truthfully and faithfully, and then write underneath it: "Portrait of a Governess, disconnected, poor and plain." And, when it is finished, your pastels can capture a second portrait — the loveliest face you can conjure: a woman not only of beauty but of titled rank and, underneath that picture write, simply, "Blanche", and if, in the days to come, you should chance to think that Mr Rochester thinks well of you, take out both pictures and compare them. Then tell yourself, Jane Eyre, that Mr Rochester might probably win the heart of the lovely lady — but is it even possible that he would waste so much as a moment's thought on the plain-face household servant?

Snap off spotlight on Jane. Bring up Lights on:

SCENE 16

The Drive, Thornfield Hall

Mrs Fairfax enters, flustered, at one side of the stage as John hastens on, excitedly, from the other

John They're coming, ma'am.
Mrs Fairfax Where are they now?

John Just passed through Millcote — I caught sight of the coach as it came over the hill — they'll be arriving any minute!

Mrs Fairfax See that the groom is ready for them — then come back quickly and help Kitty with the luggage.

John goes off as Kitty, a maid, enters

Are the bedrooms aired and have they all fresh linen?

Kitty There's warming-pans between clean sheets, ma'am, and Cook says to tell you that the baby lamb is well-nigh roasted and will half-past seven suit for the soup?

Mrs Fairfax Tell Cook she must needs serve up Lord Ingram's dinner when Lord Ingram wants it — not when it best suits Cook. Not now, Kitty! They're here.

Over which, Jane and Adele, and such members of the household staff as can be mustered are gathered at one side to watch the arrival of the visitors. There will be the usual to and fro'ing of Servants bearing in the luggage

Lord Ingram, a foppish man in his mid-twenties, enters with his mother, the Dowager Lady Ingram who has "an expression of almost insuperable haughtiness". They are accompanied by their elder daughter, Mary, who is as muddle-headed as her brother

Lady Ingram The next time I go anywhere by coach, Theo, I shall not go by coach — if I deign to *go* at all, but follow Blanche's and Mr Rochester's example and travel behind the vehicle on horseback.

Lord Ingram There are more than thirty miles between Gorstone Hall and Thornfield, Mamma — and I fear that horse-riding is a young person's prerogative.

Lady Ingram And travelling by coach is a punishment for the aged. A saddle, at least, is fashioned to fit one's figure — that coach-seat is as hard and flat as a poor-house bench!

Mary It's true, Theo. I swear that coachman went out of his way to jolt us along every rutted cart-track he could lay wheel to. I would have ridden with Blanche and Mr Rochester myself, had Blanche not intimated that my company wasn't wanted.

As Lord and Lady Ingram and Mary move on, past Jane, Adele and the group of Servants, into the house, Rochester and Blanche enter

Blanche (*answering something Rochester has said*) But I prefer a grown man's company, Mr Rochester — I find young men today poor, puny things, not fit to stir a step beyond papa's gates — nor even to go that far without Mamma's permission! Young men displease me.

Rochester I give thanks to God then, madam, that I do not fit into that category — for to suffer a frown from you would be sufficient substitute for capital punishment.

It is Rochester's and Blanche's turn to move past Jane, Adele and the Servants and into the house, as the Lights fade and come up immediately on:

Scene 17

Thornfield Hall

Where Jane and Adele are sitting on the floor, downstage and to one side, as Lord Ingram, Lady Ingram, Blanche, Mary and Rochester enter

During the following Mary sits on the cushion c where she is joined by Lord Ingram who has a box of expensive chocolates which he shares with his sister

Blanche Whose is the little puppet over there?

Mary Won't she be Mr Rochester's ward? The little French girl that he told us of?

Blanche Mr Rochester, I thought that you were not fond of children?

Rochester Nor am I.

Blanche Then what induced you to take charge of such a little doll as the one over there? Where did you pick her up?

Rochester I did not pick her up. She was left on my hands.

Blanche You should have sent her to school.

Rochester I could not afford it—schools are dear.

Blanche But governesses do not come cheap, Mr Rochester, and I felt sure I saw one in attendance. Yes, there she is! I should imagine that you are obliged to pay this person? I cannot but think that a governess comes more expensive than sending a child to school? More so, for you also have her to clothe and feed.

Rochester I have never given the matter a moment's thought.

Lady Ingram Nor ever will, I suppose. You men never do consider economy and common sense.

Blanche You should hear mamma on the subject of governesses.

Lady Ingram Don't ask me to speak upon the subject — simply to consider them affords me nervous palpitations. The time I wasted in interviewing, employing and dispensing with their services! We had a German governess once, Mr Rochester, a large strict woman. Theodore never quite recovered from that person's ministrations. Did you, Theo?

Lord Ingram Did you speak, Mamma?

Lady Ingram You see? I have been a martyr to the incompetence and caprice of governesses. I only thank heaven that I am not required to concern myself with them any longer.

Jane, who is within earshot of all of the above, is wracked with humiliation

Mary Mamma! She's listening.

Lady Ingram (*flashing Jane a disparaging glance*) *Tant pis!* I hope she is. I trust that she may have heard something that may prove of benefit. I have been studying her carefully. I am an excellent judge of a person's character, Mr Rochester, by their physical appearance — and in hers I see all the defects of her class.

Rochester And what are they, madam?

Lady Ingram I will whisper them in your ear. Or, better still, ask Blanche. I am sure that she could tell you and she is nearer to you than I.

Blanche Pray, do not refer him to me, Mamma! I have one word and one word only on the entire subject of governesses: they are a nuisance.

Lady Ingram My lily-flower, as always, you are absolutely right.

Mary We used to tease some governesses dreadfully, didn't we, Tedo?

Lord Ingram guffaws

Do you remember Madame Joubert? We tormented the very life out of that woman. We had her in tears — I can see her now. You remember those days, Tedo?

Lord Ingram Yes, to be sure I do!

Mary We drove her to distraction.

Lord Ingram No more than the cantankerous crone deserved —
attempting to teach such clever blades as we were, when she herself was
such a common ignoramus.

Blanche I remember Madame Joubert — a small, plain, ordinary person,
wasn't she?

Mary Particularly plain.

Lord Ingram Extremely ordinary.

Blanche I often consider it peculiar, how looks are so important to a
woman — a plain woman is a blot on the fair face of creation — and yet
mean nothing in a gentleman. The reverse, if anything. After all, when
I marry, I don't want a husband who is my rival, but a foil to me. When
I walk into a room on his arm, I want all eyes to be on me, not him.

Rochester If you were to marry Adonis, madam, it would be his lot to go
through life unnoticed.

*The attention no longer on her, Jane slips out of the room, taking Adele
with her. She moves downstage to the piano*

Jane's exit goes unnoticed by everyone save Rochester

Blanche And if, as payment for that pretty compliment, I were to offer to
play for you — would you sing for me?

Rochester I could not refuse. But in a moment, if you will excuse me. I
thought I heard a carriage in the drive.

*As the Lights fade on the drawing room Lord Ingram, Lady Ingram,
Blanche and Mary move across to group around the piano. Rochester
moves downstage where he encounters Jane who is attempting to avoid
him*

Rochester Jane? How are you?

Jane I am very well, sir.

Rochester What have you been doing while I've been absent?

Jane Nothing particular. Teaching Adele as usual.

Rochester And getting a good deal paler than when I saw you last. What's
wrong?

Jane Nothing at all, sir.

Rochester Did you catch a chill that night you saved my life?

Jane Not in the least.

Rochester Come back into the drawing room.

Jane I am tired, sir.

Rochester And more than a little sad. Tell me why?

Jane Nothing, nothing, sir. And I am not sad at all.

Rochester But I say that you are — and so much sad that it would take little more to bring tears into your eyes. Indeed, they are there now as we speak, shining and swimming. Speak now before we give food for gossip to some passing servant. Jane, tell me quickly ——

Jane Sir, I——

They move apart as Mrs Fairfax enters. Jane exits

Mrs Fairfax Sir, there is a gentleman to see you.

Rochester I am expecting no-one. Who is he?

Mrs Fairfax He has been here before, sir, when you were away. He would not give his name then, sir, and neither will he now.

Richard Mason enters. He is in his mid-thirties and of a nervous disposition

Mason Rochester.

Rochester Mason? But you are overseas, man.

Mason I was — until a month ago. I deemed it best to keep my identity to myself until you and I were face to face.

They shake hands — but more like adversaries before a fight than friends

Mrs Fairfax goes off in one direction as Rochester, after glancing towards the drawing-room, leads Mason off in another

Rochester This way.

The Lights come up slowly again on the drawing-room and the group gathered at the piano which is lit by a candelabra. Mary is seated at the piano where she has located a piece of sheet music

Mary Here's an odd piece!

She plays a couple of introductory bars of the "Poor Orphan Child" theme. Then, as she plays the chorus, Blanche and Lord Ingram join in the song

Lord Ingram   Why did they send me so far and so lonely,
Blanche   Up where the moors spread and grey rocks are pil'd?
Mary   Men are hard-hearted and kind angels only
                       Watch o'er the steps of the poor orphan child...

Lord Ingram guffaws at the banality of the song. The others join him in laughter. But the sound of their laughter is drowned by a scream coming from somewhere in the house. The Lights fade but come up immediately on:

SCENE 18

Thornfield Hall

Which is in shadow as Rochester, holding a single candle, hustles in Mason who, we will discover, is bleeding badly at the shoulder. Without a word, Rochester guides Mason to the one solitary chair which is set, C. *John, also holding a candlestick, appears on the gallery, looking down into the shadows*

John What is it? What's wrong?
Rochester (*calling up*) Nothing's amiss, man. Get back upstairs.
John My missis said, go down, sir — she's up there now with her head deep down under the bed-clothes.
Rochester Then go back now and assure her — assure everyone, guests and servants, there is nothing untoward.

As John hurries off, Lord Ingram arrives on the gallery, in his dressing-gown, also with a candle and nervously brandishing a pistol

Lord Ingram Is it robbers, Rochester? I've told the gels to lock their jewel boxes and themselves inside Mamma's room for safekeeping.
Rochester It is no more than a rehearsal for *Much Ado About Nothing*, sir. A servant in the west wing suffered a nightmare. The ladies may sleep safe and soundly in their beds.
Lord Ingram A servant, sir? Suffered a nightmare! In my opinion, for what it's worth, a servant that suffers nightmares, sir, is a servant that's too well fed!

As Lord Ingram exits bad-temperedly, Rochester beckons Jane, who has recently arrived, out of the shadows. She is carrying a bowl of water, bandages, a sponge and some smelling salts

Rochester You have fetched everything I asked for? Sponge? Bandages? Smelling salts?
Jane Yes, sir.
Rochester You don't turn sick, Jane, at the sight of blood?
Jane I think I shall not — I have never been tested.
Rochester Then give me your hand — best not to risk a fainting fit.

Jane gives him her hand

Warm and steady. Over here.

He leads her across to where Mason is sitting, slumped in the chair, a shirt-sleeve soaked in blood

You are all right?

Jane nods

Take this then.

Rochester gives her the candle, taking the bowl, bandages, etc., from her. He puts them down beside the chair then rips open Mason's shirt to reveal the bleeding gash on his shoulder

Jane What happened to him? Will he recover?
Rochester (*ignoring the first question*) No doubt of it. It is by no means fatal — but I must staunch the bleeding and get him to a surgeon.

Rochester slaps Mason's cheek, reviving him to consciousness. Mason looks around, fearfully

Mason She's done for me.
Rochester Not a whit. Give it a fortnight and you'll not be a pin worse for the encounter.

Rochester cleans the wound with water and a sponge during the following

Mason She bit me, Rochester! She was like an animal!

Rochester I warned you. You should not have gone near her on your own.

Mason I thought I might do some good.

Rochester (*impatiently*) Thought! Thought!

Mason She seemed so calm at first. She sucked at the blood! She howled
at me! I swear she meant to drain my heart!

Rochester Hold your tongue, man! Forget her gibberish — and for all our
sakes, hers not least, I pray you, don't repeat it.

Mason I wish to God I could forget it!

Rochester You will — once you are out of the country. Then you may
think of her as dead and buried — or, better still, never give thought to
her at all.

Mason I shall never be able to put this night from my memory!

*Mason closes his eyes, as if trying to blot out the night's events, and lapses
again into unconsciousness. Rochester, having cleaned the wound, is
holding the sponge against it to stem the flow of blood*

Rochester It will soon be morning too — and I needs must get him to a
surgeon before the house begins to stir. Will you stay with him while I
put a horse in the chaise? And sponge the blood if it starts up again?

Jane If that is what you would have me do, sir.

Rochester I would also have you keep your silence while I am gone —
and give me your assurance that you will not speak to him on any pretext.
Mason!

Mason's eyes flicker open

If you so much as say a single word to this girl while I'm away, it will
be at peril of your life. Is that understood? Open your lips, sir, and I will
not answer for the consequences.

Jane takes hold of the sponge

Jane, you are a mercy to me.

Narrator This done, he moved with a slow step and abstracted air towards a door in the wall bordering the orchard.

The Lights fade and come up immediately on:

Scene 19

The Garden, Thornfield Hall

As dawn comes up to the sound of birdsong, Rochester enters

Rochester Jane!

Jane, who has been walking in the garden, enters, with her shawl over her shoulders

Rochester Mrs Fairfax said you'd come outside. Are you the same as me — do you find the house as oppressive as a dungeon?

Jane On the contrary, in general, I am very happy when I am inside its walls. How is the gentleman?

Rochester In excellent hands. But he will not be coming back here when he's recovered.

Jane And will Grace Poole remain here still?

Rochester If you trust me, Jane, you will put last night's episode out of your thoughts.

Jane And the night she set your bed ablaze as well? It seems to me that so long as she is in your house your life is in danger.

Rochester Jane — whenever my life is in turmoil, it seems that yours also gets involved. Do you hate me for it?

Jane Hate you? No, sir. I like to serve you — and to obey you in all that is right.

Rochester (*taking her hand*) What cold fingers. They were warmer last night when I held them.

Jane (*snatching her hand away*) I think we should talk of the future, sir, not of what is past.

Rochester What about the future ?

Jane I have as good as been informed, sir, that you are shortly going to be married.

Rochester Yes. And?

Jane In that case, sir, Adele should go to school and I must advertise for a new position elsewhere.

Rochester Advertise?

Jane I am sure that you must see the necessity of that.

Rochester Advertise! You shall walk up the pyramids of Egypt first! At your peril you will advertise!

Jane Yes, sir. I shall advertise immediately. Meantime, I suppose that I may stay here? Until I find another shelter to take myself to.

Rochester Lady Ingram knows of a situation that I think would suit — in Connaught, Ireland.

Jane It is a long way off, sir.

Rochester But a girl of your spirit will not object to the voyage or the distance.

Jane No, sir — but the sea will seem a huge barrier.

Rochester A barrier from what, Jane?

Jane From England — and from this house — and from ...

Rochester Well?

Jane From you, sir. It is a long way. I hate the thought of leaving here. I have been happier here than I have ever been. I have met you, Mr Rochester, and it frightens me — terrifies me — to feel that I must go away and never set eyes on you again. I know that I have to go — I know it as surely as I know that one day I shall die — and, at this moment, I think that I would rather die than go away from here.

Rochester Then why go?

Jane Because you give me no option, sir.

Rochester What have I done?

Jane How can I stay here and know that I mean nothing to you? What must you think of me? What *do* you think of me? Do you think that I am entirely bereft of feelings? Because I am what I am — because I have no money and because I'm plain — that I'm also lacking a soul — a heart? Because this much I will say, Mr Rochester, if God had given me half Blanche Ingram's looks — let alone her station — I should have made it just as hard for you to turn your back on me as it is for me to walk away from you. I wish to God we could have met as equals.

Rochester But we are equals, Jane. (*He takes her in his arms and tries to kiss her*) Give me your mouth.

Jane (*struggling free*) No, sir — no! You are a married man — as good as — not only that, but marrying someone who is in no way your equal. An idle empty-headed woman. I know that you have no regard for her. Why then? I couldn't even contemplate marrying someone I had no regard for. No, we are not equals, Mr Rochester. Oh, but you misjudge me. You misjudge me and you underestimate me. I am a human being and with a mind of my own.

Rochester Be free to use it then, Jane. Make up your mind and decide your destiny. I offer you my heart. I offer you my hand. I offer you half of everything I own.

Jane Don't try to play games with me.

Rochester No game — I'm asking you to go through life, your hand in mine.

Jane How can you — when you have already made that self-same offer to someone else? Shall there be three of us then, walking hand-in-hand, along life's by-ways?

She turns her back on him

Rochester Jane? Jane! Come here. Turn to me. At least let's talk as friends to one another. Look at me, Jane! Turn to me! I order you to look at me!

Jane Your bride-to-be stands between us.

Rochester My bride-to-be stands before me. She is my equal — she is myself — my flesh — my very being. Jane, will you marry me?

Jane (*turning to him; slowly*) If you meant it, sir...

Rochester Jane, I swear it to you!

Jane Do you truly love me?

Rochester Yes! I ache for you.

Jane And sincerely want me for your wife?

Rochester More than I want for anything on God's earth or under the sun.

Jane Then, yes — yes, sir, I will marry you.

Rochester Say "Edward". Give me my name. Let me hear it: "Edward, I will marry you."

Jane Dear Edward — yes, yes! — Edward, yes, I will marry you, yes, and happily with all my heart.

Rochester Then come to me. Come to me entirely. (*He takes her in his arms and kisses her gently*) Dearest Jane. Jane Eyre — soon to be Jane Rochester. In four weeks, Jane, and not one day longer, you shall be my wife.

He smothers her face with kisses before kissing her hungrily on the mouth and she replies with equal passion. As the Lights darken, we hear again the sound of mocking laughter

The Lights come up on the impending wedding scene downstage. Mrs Fairfax crosses with her arms full of fresh-picked flowers. John crosses with several brace of game. Leah crosses with a dress-box which contains Jane's wedding dress. During all this, the bed is set c, for the next scene. Finally, Rochester enters downstage, in his topcoat, hat and carrying his riding-crop, as Mrs Fairfax returns

Mrs Fairfax Welcome home, sir.
Rochester Where is Miss Eyre?
Mrs Fairfax She waited up for your return, sir — she was so eager and excited — and finally retired to her room. It has been a long day for her and a longer day is in front of her tomorrow — and, if you'll excuse me, Mr Rochester, there's a dozen and one things yet that I have to attend to for the wedding: the salmon that was promised faithfully never came; the game that did come had not long been hung ——

Kitty crosses with the flowers now arranged in a vase

Not in the drawing-room, Kitty, those are intended for the morning-room — I'll show you where...

Mrs Fairfax and Kitty exit. The Lights fade

Rochester crosses to the following scene as the Lights come up on:

SCENE 20

Jane's Bedroom, Thornfield Hall

This is represented solely by a single bed in the warm glow of candlelight

Rochester Jane!
Jane (*off*) Who's there?
Rochester I am home, Jane!
Jane (*off*) One moment.

Jane enters, in her night-gown, and with her hair down

Rochester I had thought to find you waiting for me. Have you not missed me?

Jane I have missed you, sir — and, oh, how I have missed you! I have wanted you. But I had thought to keep you waiting for a glimpse of me until you take me into church tomorrow.

Rochester (*sitting on the bed*) The rain has stopped. It has turned into a cool but pleasing night. How is my Jane?

Jane As you can see, sir — the night is serene and so am I.

Rochester Are you ready for tomorrow?

Jane More than ready.

Rochester And after the service I shall whisk you away. A brief stay in town and then off to regions nearer to the sun: Paris, Rome, Naples ... all of the ground I have previously wandered over as a footloose bachelor — I shall revisit with an angel for companion.

Jane I am not an angel. I will bemyself. Mr Rochester, you must not expect anything celestial of me, any more than I shall expect the same of you. We must neither of us be disappointed in the other.

Rochester What do you expect of me?

Jane For a while, I expect you to be as you are now— but only for a little while — and then, I think, you will turn cool — and then I will not know what to think of you for a time and I shall find it hard to please you. But when you have got used to me, and being with me, perhaps you will begin to like me — like me, I say, not love me. Love will come later.

Rochester What? And do you suppose that I don't love you now? Come here — I'll prove to you how much I love you.

Jane No, sir. I would rather be excused.

Rochester There is some flint in you, miss! You have behaved like this these past few weeks: as slippery as an eel and thorny as a briar-rose. I have not been able to lay a finger anywhere without getting pricked.

Jane Perhaps I have behaved intentionally so, sir — for there is more to me as you must surely learn, than soft compliant womanhood — and it is only fair that you should know what sort of bargain you have struck, before it is too late to go back on it.

Rochester Believe me, Jane, wild horses would not keep me from the church tomorrow.

Jane Good. Then after tomorrow, sir, we shall never close the door to the bedroom on one another again. (*She takes his hand and she guides him, gently but firmly from the bed towards the door*) But until that happy time arrives, I must bid you a very dear good-night, sir.

Rochester (*bemused*) Good-night to you, Jane.

Rochester exits

Jane continues to the audience

Jane I love him more than life itself — but I will not allow my marriage to founder in a sea of sentiment. It has not been easy, these past few weeks, for it has kept him rather silent and moody — he is becoming my entire world — but if we are to spend our lives together, not just as wife and husband but as equal partners, there must be more to marriage than tender words and kisses — for while there is a place for both of those, there is room also for serious conversation and mutual respect.

Jane gets into bed. The Lights grow dim and she sleeps fitfully

Bertha Mason arrives at the bedside. She is wearing Jane's wedding veil over her hair which, as always, hangs over her face. She wears the same grubby shapeless night-gown as before. Kneeling by the bed, she puts out a hand and touches Jane's face

(Half-asleep still) Leah, what are you doing?

Bertha Mason continues to explore Jane's face with fluttering fingers

Leah? Leah?

Jane wakens at last, sees the curious figure at her bedside and leaps out. Then, cowering with fear, gazes across the bed at the uninvited stranger. Bertha Mason slowly lifts the veil from off her head and rips it in two pieces. Finding voice at last, Jane screams

Black-out

ACT II

SCENE 1

Thornfield Hall

This is represented by a single chair on which Jane, still wearing her night-gown, is sitting. Rochester stands behind the chair. Mrs Fairfax, Leah and Grace Poole stand in front of Jane. It is early morning

Rochester It was not Mrs Fairfax?

Jane shakes her head

It was not Leah, you say?

Jane shakes her head again

And it was not Mrs Poole?

Jane No, sir. Most certainly, it was not Mrs Poole.

Rochester And not one of you ladies saw or heard anything untoward last night?

Mrs Fairfax Apart from hearing Miss Eyre cry out sir, nothing. And then, when there was no further sound, I took it that she must have suffered a nightmare, sir, and went back to sleep myself.

Rochester A wise assumption, it would seem, Mrs Fairfax.

Grace I peered out into the corridor, sir, when I heard the scream, but there was no-one there and I can swear to that.

Leah I never heard nothing, Mr Rochester. Not even Miss Eyre's shouting out — but then my room's not so close to hers, besiding which, once I drops off, you could drive a coach and horses through my bedchamber and I wouldn't so much as stir.

Rochester Thank you, ladies. You may go about your duties — there's a busy day ahead for all of us.

Grace and Leah bob obsequiously and exit in separate directions

Mrs Fairfax With regard to the arrangements, sir, when you and Miss
  Eyre ... Mrs Rochester, as she will be then, return from the church?
Rochester See to it that our luggage is brought down from our rooms.
Mrs Fairfax Very good, sir.
Rochester You might arrange some breakfast too, directly.
Mrs Fairfax I'll attend to that, sir.

Mrs Fairfax goes out

Jane It was no dream I suffered last night, Edward, and I can willingly
  swear to that.
Rochester In which case, Jane, and if it was also not a servant that came
  into your room — then who, or what do you suggest it was? A ghost
  perhaps?
Jane Perhaps. I certainly never saw a living face like that before. The
  figure had thick, dark hair hanging long down its back — and a savage
  face with deep-set bloodshot eyes blazing under thick black eyebrows.
Rochester A savage face, you say, with deep-set eyes — aren't ghosts
  usually described as pale, translucent things?
Jane It was not a dream, sir.
Rochester And not a ghost and not a living person that either of us has
  ever before set eyes upon — and yet you saw it.
Jane Yes!
Rochester In your room.
Jane Leaning over me as I awoke and with the veil I was to wear today
  thrown over its head — staring down at where I lay.
Rochester And then?
Jane And then it took the veil from off its head and ripped it hard apart.
  And then I screamed out loud and fainted — for the second time in my
  life, I lost consciousness out of sheer, stark terror.
Rochester And after you had recovered consciousness, the thing had
  vanished?
Jane It was no longer there — whatever it was.
Rochester What did you do?
Jane I got out of bed. I bathed my face. I took a drink of water. I was quite
  calm. I had no fever. What I had seen, I knew that I had seen it with both
  of these eyes. I did not dream it, Edward.

Rochester Perhaps not — and then again, perhaps. I doubt that we shall ever know the truth of the matter.

Jane I know. I know it was no dream. (*She opens her hands to reveal that she has been clutching the two halves of the veil*) Is this a dream? Did a dream cause this to happen?

Rochester (*taking the veil from her*) Thank God it was only the veil that suffered.

Jane I did dream a dream last night, Edward, a nightmare that seemed as real and awful, almost, as the awful reality that followed it.

Rochester Yes?

Jane I dreamed that Thornfield Hall was gone — except for a ruined shell — a place of rats and bats and owls. I dreamed that it was a moonlit night and that I was wandering through empty walls, wrapped in a shawl, looking for you and carrying a little child in my arms — a child that I could not — must not — put down, no matter how heavy it grew. I had to take it with me everywhere. And then I heard a horse as it galloped off into the distance. I was sure that it was your horse — and that you were going away, far away, for a great many years. I had to see you before you went. I tried to climb an ivy-covered wall, but the branches gave way beneath me. The child was clinging to me, its arms grippped around my neck in terror. And then, at last, I managed to struggle to the top — and I could see you then, astride the horse but hardly more than a speck in the distance. There was a high wind — a wind so strong that it shook the very stones the wall was built from — and then the wall crumbled away beneath me and I clutched at the child and I, too, lost my balance and I fell — and then I awoke.

Rochester And that was when you saw the creature in your room?

Jane And that was when I saw the creature in my room.

Rochester The dream was but a dream, Jane.

Jane It seemed so real!

Rochester Thornfield Hall is here. It is no ruin. And I am here and wild horses would not drag me from your side — leave alone that I would ride away of my own free will and leave you. Would I go away without a kiss? Without so much as a word?

Jane Not at this moment.

Rochester Not ever, Jane, not ever. Why, this is the day on which we are to be joined together for all time and once we are man and wife, Jane Eyre, there will be no more of these wild nightmares, that I promise you.

Jane And what of that which was not a dream, sir?

Rochester After we have been married for a year and a day, Jane, I promise I will tell you. But not now. Let us not waste a moment longer. Let Leah help you to dress quickly and then let us go to church and quit this place.

Jane I cannot go to church without something on my head.

Jane exits

Rochester calls after her. He delivers the following speech as if Jane was in a nearby ante-chamber — where for the purpose of her quick change from night-gown to wedding dress, we may assume her to be

Rochester Then choose a bonnet. There will be no-one else in church to see what you are wearing, save for the clergyman and his clerk, and I doubt that either of them will be much concerned with what you are wearing — as for myself, I shall need to look no further than your face to know that I love you. Quickly, Jane. (*He calls out to another part of the house*) John! John!

John enters

Is the luggage down?

John It is being brought down now, sir.

Rochester And the carriage ready?

John The horses are being harnessed.

Rochester Good! We shall not want it to go to church, but it must be ready and waiting the moment that we return — with boxes and luggage strapped on and the coachman in his seat.

John Yes, sir.

Rochester Is that understood?

John Yes, sir.

Rochester Then attend to it, man! Attend to it! Jane! Make haste!

John exits

Rochester remains upstage

Leah bustles in and across to another area which will represent Jane's dressing-room. Leah is holding a small substitute veil and a couple of hairpins

Leah If ever a man lacked patience!

Jane enters, wearing the wedding-dress

Leah pins on the veil

Stand still, Miss Jane, do! My hands are fair shaking with excitement as it is — I shall likely stick the pin in you, if you don't stop fidgeting. There!

Jane How is it, Leah? Will I do?

Leah You make as bonny a bride as I ever set eyes upon, Miss Jane, and that is a fact. But don't take my word for it. See for yourself.

Jane (*examining herself in an imaginary cheval mirror*) Is it me?

Adele enters

Adele Mademoiselle! Mais vous êtes très jolie!

Rochester Jane! Are you ready!

Two Narrators enter, urgently, and position themselves on either side of the stage

During the following narration Rochester takes Jane by the hand and leads her around the stage, passing Mrs Fairfax and, possibly, other Servants en route, before leading her offstage

First Narrator There was no groomsman ——

Second Narrator — no bridesmaids ——

First Narrator — no relatives to wait for or marshal——

Second Narrator — none but Mr Rochester——

First Narrator —and I.

Second Narrator Mrs Fairfax stood in the hall as we passed.

First Narrator I would feign have spoken to her ——

Second Narrator — but my hand was held by a grasp of iron.

First Narrator I was hurried along by a stride I could hardly follow.

Second Narrator To look at Mr Rochester's face was to feel that not a second of delay would be tolerated for any purpose.

As soon as Rochester has led Jane off stage, the Lights fade as we pick up on two more Narrators in the spotlight positioned on the gallery

Third Narrator I wondered what other bridegroom ever looked as he did——

Fourth Narrator —so bent up to a purpose, so grimly resolute ——

Third Narrator — or who, under such steadfast brows, ever revealed such flaming and flashing eyes.

Fourth Narrator I gazed neither on sky nor earth, my heart was with my eyes, both seemed fled into Mr Rochester's frame.

Third Narrator We entered the quiet and humble temple ——

Fourth Narrator — all was still.

The Lights fade and come up on:

SCENE 2

The Church, Thornfield

This may be represented by a pair of benches, one on either side of the aisle to represent the pews, and a pair of large, free-standing ornate candlesticks

Rochester and Jane approach and stand before the Reverend Wood—no other person appears to be present

Reverend Wood Dearly beloved, we are gathered together here in the sight of God, to join together this Man and this Woman in holy matrimony, which is an honourable estate, instituted of God in the time of man's innocency, signifying unto us the mystical union that is between Christ and his Church: and therefore is not to be by any enterprised unadvisedly, lightly or wantonly, but reverently, discreetly, advisedly, soberly and in the fear of God. Wherefore I require and charge you both, as ye will answer at the dreadful day of judgment when the secret of all hearts shall be disclosed, that if either of you know any impediment why ye may not be joined together in holy matrimony, ye do now confess it: or ye be well assured that so many who are coupled together otherwise than God's work does allow, are not joined by God, neither is their matrimony lawful. Edward Rochester, wilt thou have this

woman to be thy wedded wife ——
Briggs (*off*) The marriage cannot continue — I declare the existence of an impediment.

Jane glances around, shocked, but Rochester does not turn his head

Rochester Proceed.
Reverend Wood I cannot proceed without some investigation of this allegation — either to prove it true or false.

Briggs enters and is carrying a legal folder. The priest crosses towards him

What is the nature of this impediment? Perhaps it may be got over — explained away.
Briggs Hardly. I would say that it is insuperable, and I speak advisedly. It consists in the existence of a previous marriage. Mr Rochester already has a wife.

Jane, confused, sits on one of the benches as Rochester confronts Briggs

Rochester Who are you?
Briggs My name is Briggs. I am a solicitor in practice in Leadenhall Street in London.
Rochester And you would thrust a wife on me?
Briggs I would seek to remind you of her existence, sir, which the law recognizes, if you do not. I would further seek, sir, to jog your memory further. (*He takes an official-looking document out of his folder and begins to read*) " ... I affirm and can prove that on the twentieth of October, 1829, Edward Rochester, of Thornfield Hall, in the West Riding of Yorkshire, was married to my sister, Bertha Antoinetta, daughter of my father, Jonas, and of Antoinetta, his wife, a Creole, at St Winifred's Church, Spanish Town, Jamaica." The record of that marriage is contained in the register of that church — a copy of it is now in my possesion. This witness bears the signature of my client and is witnessed and dated.
Rochester That — if it is a genuine document ——
Briggs It has been duly testified, sir, under oath.
Rochester Then it may prove that I have previously been married — but

it does not prove that the woman named as my wife is still alive.

Briggs She was alive three months ago.

Rochester Prove it.

Briggs The gentleman who has sworn this affidavit is my witness to that fact.

Rochester Produce him then — or go to hell, man!

Briggs I will produce him first — Mr Mason, please step forward.

Mason enters

Rochester raises his fist, but succeeds in controlling his anger

Rochester What have *you* to say?

Mason's lips move soundlessly— he is too overwrought to speak

I ask you again: what do you have to say? The devil is in it if you cannot speak.

Reverend Wood Sir, sir! I would remind you that you are in the house of God. (*To Mason*) Do you stand, sir, by that sworn statement that this gentleman already has a wife and that she is living still?

Briggs Courage — speak up, Mr Mason.

Mason He has. She is. He is married to my sister and she is alive. She is at Thornfield Hall.

Reverend Wood She is not at Thornfield Hall, sir, and I would testify before God to that. I have served this parish for several years and there has never been mention of a Mrs Rochester at Thornfield Hall.

Rochester No, by God. I took care that none should hear of it — or of her. Take off your surplice — there will be no wedding on this day — or, for that matter, on any other.

The Reverend Wood takes off his vestments as Briggs brandishes his document

Briggs You admit then, do you, Mr Rochester, that the woman named herein exists?

Rochester Exists? Exists, you say? I suppose you might say that she exists — though whether she fits the description of a wife is a totally different matter. But all of that we will argue later. Briggs, Wood, Mason — I

invite you all to come up to the house and visit Grace Poole's patient.
You shall see what sort of a being I was cheated into espousing — and
also judge whether or not I had the right to break the compact — and seek
sympathy with something at least human. (*He takes Jane's hand again
and helps her to her feet*) But mark that this girl knew no more than you,
Wood, of the disgusting secret. Come, all of you — follow!

*Leading Jane by the hand, and with Wood, Briggs and Mason following,
Rochester strides out of the church and then downstage*

Two Narrators and John appear

First Narrator Still holding me fast we left the church. Three gentlemen
came after.
Second Narrator At the front door of the hall we found the carriage.
Rochester (*as the group stride past John*) John! See that the horses are
unharnessed and that the coach goes back to the coach house — it will
not be needed this day!

*Mrs Fairfax, Leah and Kitty are assembled downstage, bearing gifts, but
Rochester leads his party past them*

Back to your duties — and away with your congratulations! Who wants
them? Not I! They are fifteen years too late!
First Narrator We passed on and ascended the stairs, he still holding my
hand and beckoning the gentlemen to follow ——
Second Narrator — in a room without a window, there burnt a fire and
a lamp was suspended from the ceiling by a chain.

The Lights fade and we go to:

SCENE 3

Bertha Mason's Chamber

*We open in darkness, save for the red glow of a fire, over which Bertha
Mason is crouched, shredding a fragment of cloth in her fingers. Rochester,
Jane, Briggs, Wood and Mason have entered and at some distance. With
them our eyes become accustomed to the squalid darkness and there is*

*now sufficient light for us to make out the figure of Grace Poole, in
attendance*

Rochester Good-morning, Mrs Poole. How are you? And how is your
charge today?

Grace We're tolerable, sir, I thank you — rather snappish this morning,
but quiet enough at the moment.

Rochester (*to his companions*) That is my wife — whom I married fifteen
years ago: Bertha Mason by name and, as you can observe, she is quite
mad.

*Bertha's whimperings have given way to animal-like growls and she is
staring at Rochester through her tangled mass of hair*

Grace She sees you, sir! You had best not stay!

· **Rochester** Only a few more moments, Grace — and then I am finished.
Bigamy is an ugly word — but, yes, gentlemen, I confess that I intended
bigamy. It is Fate that has out-manoeuvred me ——

Grace Look out, sir!

*Rochester has turned his back on Bertha Mason who, taking advantage of
the moment, launches herself upon him with a wild cry. Grace wrestles her
away and calms her with a gentleness that is in contrast to her physical
appearance*

Rochester I say again, gentlemen, that this was my wife. (*He turns to
Jane*) And this is what I wished to have — this young girl who stands
so grave and quiet at the mouth of hell, looking at the ravings of an
uncurable.

Mason We had better leave here.

Rochester Go to the devil.

*As Rochester, Mason, Briggs and Wood withdraw from the chamber Jane
detaches herself from the group and crosses downstage as the Lights fade
on Grace Poole and Bertha Mason*

Jane And thus Jane Eyre, who yesterday was a loved and loving bride-
to-be or so she thought herself — is again become a sad and lonely
figure. My life is empty. A Christmas frost has come at Midsummer: a
white December storm whirls over June: a frozen shroud lies over corn
and hayfield and lanes which, yesterday, blushed full of flowers, today

are pathless with untrodden snow. My hopes are dead.

The Light comes up on:

SCENE 4

The Garden, Thornfield Hall

Jane, still wearing her wedding dress, encounters Briggs and Mason

Briggs Miss Eyre, you may consider yourself clear of all blame.
Jane Do you imagine, sir, that such an announcement can ease my pain?
Mason At least your uncle may be glad to hear it, when I tell him.
Jane My uncle? Do you know him?
Mason I have enjoyed his acquaintance, on occasion, for several years. By pure good fortune, I happened to be with him — in Madeira and on my way back to Jamaica — when he received your letter, informing him of your impending marriage.
Briggs Your uncle, astonished and distressed when Mr Mason told him of the true state of affairs here, begged him to return to England with all haste — he would have come himself had he been well enough — referring him to my good offices. Thank God, for your sake, madam, that we arrived in time — if only just. There is nothing else here, is there, Mason, that need detain us?
Mason Nothing — let us be gone.

Mason and Briggs exit

Jane watches them go

Rochester enters from another direction and hesitates in approaching Jane who now turns and stands, looking at him, ruefully

Rochester I had not expected to find you like this.
Jane How had you expected to find me?
Rochester In a fury — or else in tears — or both perhaps.
Jane I had half expected that myself.
Rochester You know that I am a scoundrel, Jane?
Jane Yes, sir.

Rochester Then tell me so to my face. Don't spare me.

Jane I cannot.

Rochester Can you ever forgive me?

Mistaking her silence for forgiveness, he opens his arms, inviting her into his embrace

Jane No! Not that!

Rochester What then? What next? Do we continue to live here, under the same roof, but as strangers to one another? "That man had nearly made me his mistress". Is that what you will tell yourself? "But from this day forward, I shall be rock and ice to him." In which circumstance, Jane, I tell you: ice and rock you will become.

Jane Our situation is changed, sir, and therefore I must change to meet that situation.

Rochester Changed how? Go back to being what we were before? Myself as master, you as governess?

Jane That neither, sir. Adele must have a new governess. I cannot stay here.

Rochester Nor I, Jane. I shall find a school for her. I shall nail up the front door and lower windows. I shall give Mrs Poole two hundred pounds a year to live here with my wife — which is how you seem to choose to view the wretched creature —

Jane (*angrily*) Sir, how I choose to see her is of little consequence — it is that hatred which you carry in your heart for the poor unfortunate woman that concerns me. It is no fault of hers that she is mad.

Rochester And do you suppose it is because she is mad that I hate her?

Jane Can there be any other reason?

Rochester You misjudge me, Jane. If you were mad, do you think I should hate you?

Jane I do indeed, sir.

Rochester Then you know nothing about me. Every particle of your flesh is as dear to me as is my own — in pain and sickness it would be no less dear. Your mind is mine to treasure and, if it were crazed, it would be mine to treasure still. If you were to fly at me as wildly as that woman did this morning — claw at me, bite me — I would hold you in my arms as gently and as fondly as I have ever held you. But why must we speak of madness when all our talk should be of putting madness behind us. I have a house in the south of France: a whitewashed villa on the shores of the Mediterranean. You shall be Mrs Rochester — as long as I live there shall never be anyone but you...

Jane shakes her head

Why do you shake your head?

Jane Sir, you already have a wife. You have acknowledged that fact this morning.

Rochester Jane, if you love me still, you will ——

Jane Yes — *yes* ! I think I love you more at this minute than I have ever done. But that is the last time that you will ever hear me say that word. Sir, I have already told you: I must leave you.

Rochester And I tell you that you shall not!

Jane God help me!

Rochester I shall forbid it! (*Controlling his anger*) What a fool I am. I keep insisting to you that I want you for my wife — and yet I haven't told you why I believe I have the right to do so. Will you listen to me?

Jane Yes, sir, for hours if you wish it.

Rochester I only ask for minutes. Have you heard it said that my father was a greedy man?

Jane I have heard rumours to such effect since I have been here.

Rochester It was his decision that I make a wealthy marriage. When I left college, I was sent out to Jamaica where a bride had already been chosen for me. My father said nothing to me about the fact that I was marrying into money — only that my fiancée was the boast of Spanish Town for her beauty. This was no lie. But before the marriage I was seldom allowed to see her alone. I had little private conversation with her. But, being young and inexperienced, I thought I loved her. So — gross, grovelling blockhead that I was — I married her. I had been told her mother was dead — but when the honeymoon was over I soon learned the truth: she was not dead, she was locked in an asylum. And there was previous history of madness in the family. Jane, I lived with that woman, as my wife, for four years in Jamaica and each day, day by day, I watched her lose her sanity.

Jane And when she was totally mad?

Rochester Then? Then there were moments when I feared for my own sanity. There was one West Indian night in May, when I was awakened by her screaming — the air like sulphur streams, the room buzzing with mosquitoes — her curses ringing in my ears — then I knelt and took out from my trunk a brace of pistols, intending to kill myself : "This is not life, this is hell" I said — and I had every right to deliver myself from it.

Jane And yet you are still here?

Rochester I listened to the voice of Hope — telling me to bring her back to England.

Jane And after you had settled her here? What did you do? Where did you go?

Rochester What did I do? Transformed myself into a will-o'-the-wisp. Where did I go? Where didn't I go? Around the Continent mostly — it was there that I met Celine Varens — and there were other women... you think me an unprincipled rake, don't you?

Jane I don't like you as well as I have sometimes done, indeed, sir. Didn't it seem wrong to you, in the least, to live like that? First with one mistress and then with another? You talk of it now as if it were a matter of course.

Rochester It seemed so at the time — although I never thought of it as living. And then, last January, a business matter brought me back to England. One frosty winter's afternoon as I rode into sight of Thornfield Hall, I caught a glimpse of a quiet little figure, sitting all alone and on a stile — and I had no thought in the moment of what she would come to mean to me.

Jane Nor she of you.

Rochester Not even when I took a tumble, and the childish, slender creature came across and helped me to my feet. Since when Jane, you have become my very life. These months that we have been together — talking and walking together in this garden — the evenings when I have held you and kissed you ——

Jane Don't talk of these times, sir. They are dead and gone.

Rochester They are! They are! And buried. Why should we dwell upon the Past, when the Present is so much surer and the Future has all we ask and everything to offer. All that is needed, Jane, is for you to make this commitment: "I will be yours, Mr Rochester."

Jane Mr Rochester, I will *not* be yours!

Rochester Can you really mean to go one way in the world and to let me go another?

Jane I do.

Rochester (*sweeping her into his arms*) Do you mean it still?

Jane I do.

Rochester (*kissing her face, again and again*) And now? And now? And now?

Jane (*struggling to free herself*) Yes, yes — *Yes* !

Rochester (*angered, releasing her*) How can you be so frail and yet so unyielding? There is nothing of you. I could snap you in half as easily as snap a twig — and yet I cannot break your spirit to my will. And it is your spirit that I seek the most, Jane, and must possess. I want you to want me of your free will.

Again, he holds out his arms for her to walk into, but she evades him

You are going?

Jane I am leaving, sir.

Rochester You mean to leave me?

Jane Yes.

Rochester Jane!

Jane Mr Rochester.

Rochester Go then. But only as far as your room. And think over all that I have said. Jane, most of all, think of me.

Jane moves to leave and Rochester slumps on the garden seat. Seeing his anguish, Jane returns, kisses him on the cheek and smooths his hair

Jane God bless you, sir. God keep you from harm and wrong. And may he reward you well for all of your past kindness to me.

Jane exits as Rochester calls after her

Rochester Your love was the only reward I ever asked, Jane! Jane! *Jane*!

Jane (*off*) Farewell, Mr Rochester ——

The Lights fade and come up immediately on:

SCENE 5

Thornfield Hall

Six Narrators enter, in phalanx and moving purposefully, to form a circle, c, looking out into the audience. One of the Narrators carries a small pile of crisply ironed white garments folded over his arms. Another carries a locket. Another a ring and another a small purse containing some coins

Narrators (*in unison*) Farewell for ever!

First Narrator I never thought to sleep tonight.

Second Narrator Then, when I had put my head upon the pillow——

Third Narrator — a slumber fell upon me — nightmare took me back to childhood ——

Fourth Narrator I dreamed that I was back at Gateshead Hall——

Fifth Narrator — and locked again inside that dreaded Red Room.

Sixth Narrator — Where amidst the chill air and silence, I became aware of a flickering, trembling light ——

First Narrator — playing against its walls and furnishings.

Second Narrator Then, suddenly, at its source a shape.

Third Narrator What seemed a hand, luminous and unearthly ——

Fourth Narrator — parted the deep red damask curtains, easing aside their heavy folds.

Fifth Narrator There, before me a human form shone against the pitch night .

Sixth Narrator It gazed upon me ——

First Narrator — exquisite and welcome and spoke to my spirit ——

Second Narrator — as if it whispered in the very chambers of my heart.

Third Narrator Jane, my child, flee temptation!

Fourth Narrator Mother, I will! The dawn approached and I rose and dressed.

Jane, now changed back into her plain, simple dress and with her shawl flung over her shoulders, enters and takes up a position in the centre of the circle of Narrators, who turn to face her. During the following speech Jane spreads a shawl on the floor

Jane Thank God! And heaven be praised that July nights are short. It will not be long till dawn and it is not too early to begin to do what must be done. I must be out of the house and away from Thornfield before the sun is up. For he will send for me in the morning and I must be gone before he does, and I shall not take with me anything that is not rightly mine to take.

A Narrator hands Jane the small pile of crisply ironed white garments which he has been carrying, folded, over his arm

Some clean linen — all of this was bought and paid for out of my own money. (*She puts the linen on the outspread shawl and a second Narrator hands her a ring*) This ring is mine.

A third Narrator hands her a locket

And this locket too belongs to me. (*Both ring and locket are placed on the shawl. Jane takes off a pearl necklace from around her neck*) But the pearl necklace was a gift from him when I promised myself to him in marriage — and therefore it must stay with him. (*She places the necklace on the floor in front of the shawl*)

Another Narrator hands her a small purse and she checks the contents

Twenty shillings — which is every penny I possess. (*She slips the purse into her pocket and wraps up her worldly possessions into a bundle*) He is awake. He has not slept at all.

A spot comes up slowly on Rochester who is standing, grief-stricken, on the gallery

I have heard him, through the night, pacing his room from wall to wall. I cannot trust myself to stand face to face to him again and not to say to him: "Mr Rochester, I will love you and live with you through life till death." But that I must not do.

The Lights come up slowly to establish full morning light

The Narrators exit, slowly, and Jane moves downstage—with Rochester still held in the spotlight on the gallery. Jane, carrying her bundle, addresses the audience

I have walked for over an hour, skirting fields and lanes and hedges. It is a lovely summer morning — but I have looked neither to the rising sun, nor smiling sky. The condemned man that rides to his execution does not see the flowers that blush at him on the wayside — but thinks only of the keenness of the executioner's axe — and of the gaping grave and I have dwelt on cheerless flight and homeless wandering — and, oh, most of all, with the agony of him that I have left behind.

As Jane exits, Leah enters, upstage

Leah Miss Jane? Are you up. Miss Jane? 'Tis well past the hour.
Rochester *(calling out from the gallery)* Leah? Leah!

Leah discovers the pearl necklace on the floor and picks it up as she calls back

　　She's not downstairs neither, sir. But John reckons that the back door
　　was unbolted when he got up — and that was ever so early on.

Leah exits

Rochester is left in a single spot as he lets out a grief-stricken cry

Rochester Jane! Jane! I beg of you. Come back to me!

*As the Light fades on Rochester, Jane enters, downstage, and addresses
the audience*

Jane May you never feel what I feel now. May your eyes never shed such
　　stormy, scalding heartwrung tears as have just poured from mine. May
　　you never appeal to heaven in prayers so hopeless and so agonized as
　　have lately left my lips — and may you never, like me, become the sole
　　destroyer of that which you wholly love!

*Overcome by torment, Jane sinks to the ground as the Lights fade again
and then come up on Jane as she is joined by the six Narrators, spaced
around the otherwise empty stage*

First Narrator Two days have passed and I have been set down, here, by
　　a coachman who could not or would not take me any further, having
　　taken from me as payment every penny I possessed.
Second Narrator Not only that, but I forgot to take my bundle out of the
　　pocket of the coach where I had placed it for safe-keeping.
Third Narrator There it remains, there it must remain ——
Fourth Narrator — and I am absolutely destitute ——
Fifth Narrator What was I to do? Where to go? Oh, intolerable questions,

when there is nothing I can do and nowhere I can go .

Sixth Narrator When I must walk for miles on my weary trembling limbs before I can find human habitation——

Second Narrator — and have my pleas for sympathy refused even before they're spoken.

Third Narrator I walk for hours ——

Fourth Narrator — and just as I am about to collapse exhausted ——

Fifth Narrator — I hear a bell chime——

Sixth Narrator — a church bell ——

A bell peals off in the distance and Jane and the Narrators all turn their heads towards the sound

First Narrator Human life is near.

Second Narrator I must struggle on.

Third Narrator Strive to live and bend and toil like the rest.

Two of the Narrators assume the roles of a village Shopkeeper and a Country Girl. The Shopkeeper's wares are represented by a large wicker basket full of breadcakes. The four remaining Narrators adopt frozen postures as two pairs of gossiping village women. The Shopkeeper — a middle-aged woman — looks up as Jane approaches her

Shopkeeper Can I get thi' anything?

Jane I'd be grateful for your permission to sit for a moment in the shade.

The Shopkeeper nods a grudging acquiescence as the Country Girl approaches

Shopkeeper Yes, Rachel?

Country Girl Two pennorth of baking powder, Mrs Wrigley, for my mam.

The Shopkeeper mimes handing over the baking powder and receives payment in the same manner

Shopkeeper Tell her the ribbon man's been, at long last, if she wants to call in when she's passing.

The Country Girl moves off and freezes with the other Narrators as the Shopkeeper turns back to Jane

Have you come far?

Jane As far as I could get from where I was before.

Shopkeeper Did it have a name?

Jane Thornfield.

Shopkeeper Thornfield? I'm no wiser. Have you far to go?

Jane You wouldn't happen to know of anywhere in this neighbourhood where a servant is wanted?

Shopkeeper I couldn't say.

Jane Is there any work to be had in these parts? What do most folk do?

Shopkeeper Farm-labouring and a good many are at Mr Oliver's needle factory — then there's t'foundry.

Jane Does Mr Oliver employ women?

Shopkeeper Nay — it's men's work up there.

Jane What do the women do?

Shopkeeper Some does one thing, and some another. Poor folk must get on as they can.

Jane (*proffering a small lace-edged handkerchief*) Would you exchange me a breadcake for this handkerchief?

Shopkeeper Nay — I don't go in for that sort of carry-on.

Jane Perhaps half a breadcake?

Shopkeeper (*with a shake of her head*) And how am I supposed to know how you came by the handkerchief in the first place?

Jane (*reaching into her pocket*) I have this pair of gloves?

Dismissing Jane, the Shopkeeper turns away. Jane crosses to where the Country Girl turns as she approaches. The Country Girl is clutching something in her hands

Jane Will you give that to me?

Country Girl Mam! There's a woman wants me to give her these scraps you told me to give to t' pig!

Another Narrator unfreezes and takes on the role of a Country Woman

Country Woman Oh, go on then lass — give 'em to her. The pig wain't know no different.

The Country Girl hands Jane the scraps of food

And when tha's done it, get thyself inside — afore it starts to pelt it down.

Jane sinks down on to her knees and wolfs down the scraps then rises to her feet and moves on leaden feet, into a wind

During the following Jane stumbles off

First Narrator My strength is quite failing me.

Second Narrator I feel I cannot go much further.

Third Narrator Shall I be an outcast again this night?

Fourth Narrator In all likelihood I shall die before morning.

Fifth Narrator And why cannot I reconcile myself to the prospect of death?

Sixth Narrator Because I believe that Mr Rochester is on this earth still.

First Narrator And to die of cold when he whom I love still lives, is a fate to which I cannot passively submit.

Second Narrator I cross the marsh. I take a track which leads towards a light.

Third Narrator I put out my hand and feel a dark mass before me.

Fourth Narrator I touch the roughness of a dry-stone wall.

Fifth Narrator A white object looms before me.

Sixth Narrator It is a wicket gate. It moves on its hinges as I touch it.

First Narrator Oh, Providence — sustain me a little longer!

As the Narrators disperse, two young women, Mary and Diana Rivers, accompanied by their old servant-woman, Hannah, and carrying hymn books, move forward singing the hymn

Diana
Mary } (*together*) { Soldiers of Christ arise,
Hannah   { And put your armour on.
                             { Strong in the strength which God supplies,
                             { Through his eternal love!

SCENE 6

The Parlour, Moor House

This is represented by four upright chairs and a side-table

They complete the verse of the hymn

Diana Now let us sing Hymn three two one —

> *But before they are able to do so, St John Rivers, a tall, slender man in his late twenties, enters, supporting Jane, his arm around her waist*

St John Mary! Diana!
Diana St John, who is it?
Hannah Where has she come from?
St John I cannot tell. I found her on the door.
Hannah She does look white.
Mary As white as earth or clay. She will fall —— let her sit.

They all help Jane to a chair

Diana Perhaps a little water will restore her. Hannah, fetch some. But she's worn to nothing.
St John (*never lacking in zealous ardour*) God be praised! For surely he has guided this unfortunate's footsteps to our door!

The Lights fade, as a Narrator appears

Narrator A flame of grateful joy flickered inside — I thanked God — exhausted, I slept.

The Lights come up on the same scene as before-—except that Jane is now sitting up and nervous of disturbing St John who sits opposite her, deep in a book. Diana and Mary are also sitting. Diana rises and crosses to Jane

Diane You would be far more comfortable on the sofa, Miss Eyre. Come — you must be obedient.

Mary You must be famished too. You have scarcely eaten these past three days — and one more day in bed would not have gone amiss.

Jane I am well enough now.

Mary (*handing Jane a small breadcake*) Eat that cake to be going on with. Hannah baked it especially for you on the bottom of the oven.

As Diana and Mary serve afternoon tea, Jane wolfs down the cake — then realizes that St John is watching her over his book

St John You are very hungry.

Jane I seem to have found my appetite. I trust I shall not eat long at your expense, sir.

St John You misunderstand me. We have never shrunk from Christian charity. We should not seek to return you to your relatives or friends until you are considered fully recovered.

Jane I must tell you, sir, I am without either home or friends.

St John Are you saying that you have no-one?

Jane I am. No tie links me to any living thing.

St John A most singular position, surely, at your age?

Mary St John!

St John You have never been married? You are a spinster?

Diana Why, she can't be above seventeen or eighteen years old, St John.

Jane I am near nineteen. But I am not married. No.

St John And you say you have no parents? Where have you been living, then?

Mary You must forgive my brother, Miss Eyre — like all clergymen he has an insatiable curiosity regarding private lives.

Jane The name of the place — and of the person with whom I lived — is something which I would prefer to keep a secret.

Diana She has the right to do so, brother, if she so wishes.

St John And if I know nothing about her, or her history, I cannot help her, Diana. And you do need help, do you not?

Jane I need it and I seek it, sir. I am hopeful that someone might help me to find employment sufficent to provide me with the barest necessities of life.

St John And I am more than willing to be that person, if it is within my powers. But I cannot do so if you are not prepared to tell me something about yourself?

Diana Don't make her talk any more now, St John. Let her be at peace for a while.

St John But she will not know peace, Diana — if I am any judge of character — so long as she is dependent upon our hospitality. Is it not true, Miss Eyre, that you have no wish to be reliant upon my sister's compassion — or my charity — it is your desire to be independent of us?

Jane It is! It is! Show me how to work, or where to look for work, that is all I ask — and I do not care if it is employment in the poorest cottage. But until that time, I ask to be allowed to stay here with you — for I could not bear to spend one more night without a roof above my head.

Diana (*putting her hand on Jane's head*) Indeed you shall stay here.

Mary You shall!

St John You see, Miss Eyre, my sisters find pleasure in keeping you here — in much the same way as they would take pleasure in keeping some half-frozen sparrow that the wintry wind had blown in through a casement window. It is my intention though to help you to help yourself — and I shall endeavour to do so.

Jane I should be grateful, sir.

St John But you must understand, Miss Eyre, that I am merely the incumbent of a poor country parish. We are not a wealthy family. Our father died but a few short weeks ago and we must needs shut up this house and sell off its contents, in order to pay off his debts.

Mary Diana and myself, Miss Eyre, are soon to take up employment as governesses to families which St John has found for us on the south coast.

St John I perceive you to be a woman of taste and learning — if you are inclined to despise the day of small things, I must urge you to seek more efficient succour than such as I can offer.

Diana She has already told you, St John, that she is more than ready to do anything that she can do.

Jane I will be a dressmaker, I will be a plain workwoman, I will be a servant, a nursemaid even — if I can be no better.

St John If such is your spirit, Miss Eyre, I am proved correct: Providence has brought you here.

Jane Tell me, please.

St John When I came back to Morton, two years ago, it had no school. The children of the poor were thus denied all hope of progress.

Mary St John has already opened a school for boys.

Diane He now means to open a second school for girls.

St John Already, there is a building for that purpose, provided by a local factory-owner, with a cottage attached for the school-mistress's accommodation. The salary is thirty pounds a year. The same benefactor will pay for the education and the clothing of an orphan from the workhouse ——

Jane Mr Rivers, are you offering me the post of school-mistress?

St John If you would not find it degrading.

Jane On the contrary, sir — I thank you for the proposal, and I accept it with all my heart.

St John Your scholars will be poor girls only — cottagers' children for the most part, farmers' daughters at best. Knitting, sewing, reading and writing will be all that you will be required to teach.

Jane I understand that fully.

St John I perceive, Miss Eyre, that we have something in common — we both consider that no service degrades which can better the human race. When shall you be ready to take up the appointment?

Jane As soon as I am needed.

Mary You are only just this morning risen from a sick-bed.

Diana At least wait until you are well again.

Jane I am quite well now. I will go and look at the cottage tomorrow, Mr Rivers — and open the school, if it is ready to be opened, within the month.

St John And I shall set off immediately to see the benefactor and inform him that we have found the school-mistress.

Diane But you have not finished your tea, brother.

Mary At least wait until this weather eases off.

St John And if I let a sprinkling of rain or a gust of wind turn me aside from such an easy task, what preparation would such sloth be for the future I propose for myself?

He strides from the room as Diana and Mary sigh as they ponder on the significance of his words then, brightening, they cross to congratulate Jane

Diana But you shall remain here with us, Jane, as our guest, as long as we are here or until your cottage is ready.

Mary Indeed you shall! You shall!

*Mary and Diana embrace Jane as the Lights fade on the Rivers' parlour
and come up on:*

SCENE 7

The Girls' School, Morton

*This can be represented by a blackboard and some half-dozen small
chairs*

Jane, her back to the audience, is writing on the blackboard

First Narrator I have been here now for almost a month. Already, some
    of my pupils are showing an aptitude for copying out their letters.
Second Narrator I am hopeful of teaching some of them to read before
    they leave.
First Narrator Several of them can knit and some of them are useful with
    their needle and thread.

Jane turns to face the audience

Jane They all speak with the broadest accent of the district.

*Over which, the Narrators have turned and are now standing behind two
of the chairs, having taken on the roles of Schoolchildren. One of them
raises a hand*

Annie Please, miss?
Jane Yes, Annie?
Annie I waint be coming to school tomorrow, miss.
Jane Why not?
Annie Me Auntie Beattie's baby died in t' fever hospital, miss. They're
    off to bury it tomorrow.
Jane I'm sad to hear that, Annie. I shall expect to see you back on
    Wednesday. Hand in your slates and pencils, girls, and Alice will collect
    them in.

The Lights fade on the schoolroom but Jane is held in a spot

I shall find some happiness here, I know ... but there are moments when I cannot help but wonder, what if ... ? Supposing I had chosen another path? I might be living now in France as Mr Rochester's mistress — delirious half the time with his love — for he would — oh, yes, he would have loved me well! But what am I saying? And, more important, what am I feeling? Whether it is better, I ask, to be a slave in a fool's paradise at Marseilles — fevered with delusive bliss one hour — suffocating with both the tears of remorse and shame the next — or to be a village school-mistress, reliant upon no man, here in the heart of England ...?

The Lights come up again on the school-room

Alice I've done, miss.
Jane (*crossing and patting Alice on the head*) Good girl, Alice.
Alice Ta, miss.
Jane God bless.

Alice and Annie go

(*turning to the audience*) Yes, I know that I was right to choose principle and Christian teaching — and to have denied the foolish promptings of a frenzied moment. God directed me to the correct decision: I thank Providence for that guidance... Oh, but he did love me — as no other man could and as no other man will ever love me again ——

Jane begins to sing softly

St John enters

Jane recovers herself hastily

Jane Mr Rivers — I was not expecting anyone.
St John I am sorry if I startled you, Miss Eyre. Are you finding the work here harder than you expected?
Jane Not at all. Quite the contrary, I am getting on very well with my scholars.
St John Perhaps the accommodation is not what you have been used to?
Jane My cottage is clean and weather-proof: my furniture is sufficient

and comfortable. You may see it for yourself. I have little in the way of
hospitality, but I could brew some tea and there is bread and butter.

St John Thank you, no. I am here on a business matter. It would be best
if we were to remain where we are. But you are happy then?

Jane I am more than happy, Mr Rivers. I would remind you that it is not
long since I had nothing — I was an outcast, a beggar, a vagrant. Now
I have friends, a home, employment. Indeed, sir, I wonder at God's
goodness and the generosity of others, not least yourself. I assure you,
I am anything but sad.

St John Then I hope, with all my heart, that you decide to remain in
Morton for some months to come.

Jane It is what I mean to do. Why should I do otherwise?

St John Sometimes our circumstances suddenly alter. To be honest, Miss
Eyre, I do not know what you may choose or may not choose to do. You
have told me so little about yourself. But as to that which is in your past
— that which you hold so close to you — may I say that it is my fervent
hope that you will be guided not to yield to that same temptation as Lot's
wife — and yearn for that which you have put behind you.

Jane What makes you think that I might choose to do so?

St John I have my reasons. Also, I presume to read your thoughts, Miss
Eyre, because your face reveals a depth of sadness — an urgent longing
— akin to one I have not long since suffered from myself.

Jane One that you wish to talk about?

St John Less than a year ago, I felt sure that I had made the wrong decision
in entering the ministry. I ached for something else — an active life —
for the destiny of an artist, say, or an author, or a politician, even a
fighting man — anything, in fact, rather than the priesthood. I considered my life so empty, so meaningless, that I knew that if I could not —
did not — change it, I had no desire to go on living.

Jane And then?

St John And then, Miss Eyre, I spoke to God. Or rather, I should say, God
spoke to me. He told me that I was to fulfil an errand — one that would
not only give me a purpose in life, but would also demand of me the
individual requirements of all professions I had envied: soldier, states-
man, orator — I would need to be all of these, Miss Eyre, and more, in
order to obey his command.

Jane And which calling, Mr Rivers, requires such diversity of talents?

St John The Lord God required me to become a missionary, Miss Eyre
— and from the moment that he issued that call, I have rarely given

thought to any other matter.

Jane And yet you are not a missionary, Mr Rivers?

St John My father was opposed to it. I respected the wishes of a dying man. But now that he has gone, there is nothing to deter me in my resolve. There are some items in his will still to be settled; a new incumbent to be appointed in the parish — and then, Miss Eyre ——

There is a knock on the door, off, which seems to startle him

Jane Are *you* expecting someone?

St John I was so caught up with my own ambitions I had quite forgotten my main purpose in coming here. The business matter I mentioned when I first arrrived.

Jane Is it school business?

St John No, Miss Eyre — your own.

Another knock

One moment! A gentleman who wishes to see you. It was my suggestion that he might come here. I said earlier that your past life might catch up with you.

Jane Is it Mr Rochester?

St John No. It is not your Mr Rochester.

Briggs, the solicitor, enters

Jane Mr Briggs?

Briggs Good-afternoon, Miss Eyre.

Jane (*to St John*) You have sought out this gentleman? You have made enquiries about my life before I came here?

Briggs On, the contrary, Miss Eyre — it is I who have sought you out — and found you entirely by coincidence. Mr Rivers had approached me with regard to his late father's estate. Your name was mentioned only by chance.

Jane (*to St John*) But I have been a subject for subsequent conversation?

St John Mr Briggs has informed me of your previous employment — as governess to the ward of Edward Rochester.

Jane Mr Rivers!

Briggs I appreciate your concern, Miss Eyre, but hear me to the end. I deemed it no less than my duty to inform Mr Rivers of the facts concerning our previous encounter: that Edward Rochester professed to offer you an honourable marriage and, at the very altar, you learned that there already was a wife. That you yourself were totally innocent in this proposed deceit.

St John He must have been an evil man.

Jane Mr Rivers, you know nothing about him. Don't seek to offer false opinions. (*To Briggs*) How is he? What is he doing? Is he well?

Briggs shakes his head and shrugs

But you have been to Thornfield Hall? You must have seen him?

Briggs No. I have merely corresponded.

Jane What did his letters say? Who has them? May I see them?

Briggs The reply received, in answer to my query, did not come from Mr Rochester but from Mrs Alice Fairfax. My interest was in you, not in your previous employer.

Jane What do you want with me?

Briggs To inform you, Miss Eyre, that your uncle, Robert Sumner Eyre, who was resident in Madeira, is dead. You are his only living relative and heiress to all of his fortune. You are rich, Miss Eyre.

Jane I am? Rich?

Briggs There are some small bequests to be deducted — but, when everything has been added up or taken away, you will receive somewhere in the nature of twenty thousand pounds.

Jane You are right. It is a fortune. There is no mistake?

Briggs There is no mistake, Miss Eyre.

Jane Perhaps you have read the figures wrong? It may be two thousand?

Briggs (*producing the legal document from out of his folder*) It is written in letters, not figures. (*He shows her the relevant paragraph*) Twenty thousand pounds. With your permission, I shall take my leave of you, Miss Eyre, and give you time to digest your change in fortune. I have other business matters to attend to in the district and shall be here for several days. I shall call on you again before I leave. If you would care for my office to act on your behalf, I shall be more than happy to attend to it. You do not need to make that decision now. Mr Rivers, Miss Eyre...

Briggs goes out

Jane paces the room eagerly

Jane Oh, I am glad. I am glad! Did you know about this? Are you glad for me?

St John I knew that you had been mentioned in your uncle's will. I did not know that it amounted to a fortune. The news comes as more of a shock, I think, to me than to yourself — for I cannot adhere to the thought that wealth, of a necessity, brings happiness. For myself, I would fear the opposite — I aspire only after the day when I shall ascend to my Lord, knowing I have sought my salvation in the paths of poverty and obscurity. I am pleased, for your sake, that this wealth has come your way — but I cannot say that I am entirely without reservation. But if you are glad ...

Jane Not for myself, St John. I am glad for what this inheritance will help me to do. Think of it! We shall all spend Christmas together. We shall send for Mary and Diana from the south of England. There will be you, there will be me, there will be Hannah. We shall open up Moor House again.

St John Moor House is not ours to open. It is up for sale.

Jane Good! I shall buy it back. No, *we* shall buy it back, for it shall belong to all of us.

St John Tell me where I can get you a glass of water? You really must make an effort to tranquillize your feelings.

Jane Nonsense! You quite put me out of patience. I am rational enough.

St John You are acting on first impulses. You must take days even to consider such a matter — and then discuss it with your lawyer.

Jane Not when I am incapable of considering any other. I am resolved that I shall have a home and connections — these are all that I have ever wanted. I like Moor House: I like Diana and Mary — and I will attach myself for life to them. And it shall be your home too. When you are done with wandering.

St John But it is your fortune, Jane. You owe us nothing.

Jane I owe you everything. I would have died that night, had you not taken me in and were you to argue with me for a year I could not deny myself the delicious pleasure of repaying, in part, a mighty obligation and winning myself lifelong friends.

St John You think so now because you have not yet fully grasped your situation. Because you do not know what it is to possess twenty thousand pounds. You cannot have a notion of the importance which twenty thousand pounds will give you.

Jane And you cannot imagine the craving, the need I have for fraternal love. I never had a home, I never had a family — don't try to deny me that which I crave for most in the world.

St John But, Jane, your aspirations after family ties and happiness may be otherwise realized. You may meet someone and marry.

Jane Nonsense! Marry? I don't want to marry. I shall never marry. My mind is made up. I know exactly what I mean to do...

The Lights fade and come up on:

SCENE 8

The Parlour, Moor House

Three Narrators enter, briskly, as the school furniture is removed and the Moor House chairs and table set behind them

During the following Hannah enters and spreads out a tablecloth and goes out

First Narrator My first aim will be to clean down Moor House from chamber to cellar.

Second Narrator My next to rub it up with beeswax, oil and an indefinite number of cloths until it glitters.

Third Narrator Afterwards I shall attempt to drive us all close to ruin in coals and peat to keep up good fires in every room.

First Narrator Lastly, the few days left to me before your sisters come back home will be devoted by Hannah and myself to such a beating of eggs ——

Second Narrator — sorting of currants ——

Third Narrator — grating of spices ——

First Narrator — compounding of Christmas cakes ——

Second Narrator — baking of mince-pies ——

Third Narrator — and solemnizing of other culinary rites, as words can convey.

Hannah now brings in Christmas cake, cheese, pastries, etc.

St John enters carrying a candelabra holding several lit candles which serve to bathe the scene in a warm and festive glow. Jane accompanies him

Several Carol-Singers gather on stage outside the Moor House

Against the background of the singing, St John and Jane continue their conversation

Carol Singers   God rest ye merry, gentlemen,
                      Let nothing you dismay,
                      For Jesus Christ our saviour
                      Was born upon this day
                      To save us all from Satan's power
                      When we were gone astray:
                      O tidings of comfort and joy,
                      Comfort and joy,
                      O tidings of comfort and joy!

St John And now that you are a woman of means, must the school be closed?

Jane I will stay on, after Christmas, until you have found someone to replace me.

St John And what will you do then, Jane? What aim, what purpose will you have then in life? Will you have no ambitions further than domestic endearments and household joys?

Hannah peers off

Hannah They're coming! They're coming!

Jane (*in answer to St John's questions*) The best thing the world has.

Diana and Mary enter. They are dressed for travelling and are carrying cloth-covered wicker baskets. During their embraces as they greet each other, St John kisses both of his sisters

Diana St John, it is Christmas — and Jane has been more than a sister to all three of us — you should kiss her too!

St John approaches Jane, places his hands on her shoulders and kisses her gently on the mouth. It is a meaningful moment which is held as they look into each other's eyes, and which is broken as Hannah looks inside the cloth-covered baskets which Diana and Mary have brought with them

Hannah Oysters!
Diana And lobsters.
Mary Fresh yesterday from Whitstable.

The Carol-singers have reached the end of their first chorus. St John and Jane reprise the closing lines, still holding each other's glance

St John }   (*singing*)   ⎧ O tidings of comfort and joy,
Jane   }   ⎨ Comfort and joy,
                                        ⎩ O tidings of comfort and joy!

As Hannah hands round hot punch and Christmas cake, the Carol-singers enter the parlour as they reprise

Carol-singers
God rest ye merry Gentlemen,
Let nothing you dismay,
For Jesus Christ our saviour
Was born upon this day,
To save us all from Satan's power
When we were gone astray:
O tidings of comfort and joy,
Comfort and joy,
O tidings of comfort and joy!

The Lights fade and come up on:

SCENE 9

A Moorland Glen, near Morton

A sunny spring evening, as Jane and St John enter

St John Let us rest here.

Jane sits on the ground but St John remains standing

I asked you to accompany me this evening, Jane, because there is something that I wanted to discuss with you. I have made my final arrangements. I sail on the twentieth of June.

Jane God will protect you, St John — for you have undertaken His work.

St John Yes, there is my glory and my joy. Jane, come with me to India. Forswear your wealth — bequeath it to charity. Come as my helpmate and my humble fellow-labourer.

Jane (*scrambling to her feet*) Oh, St John! Have some mercy!

St John God intended you for a missionary's wife. A missionary's wife you must be — shall be.

Jane I am not fit for it.

St John Who is?

Jane I have no vocation.

St John Jane, I have watched you — studied you — ever since we met. You have all the qualities for it, and more. You are diligent, faithful, constant, courageous, gentle and heroic. I can trust you unreservedly.

Jane Seek one elsewhere than in me, St John.

St John It is what I want. Jane, you would never regret marrying me.

Jane Supposing I were to say that, yes, I will go with you — but as your fellow-missionary, not as your wife?

St John How can you say that?

Jane Because I cannot marry you and become part of you.

St John But that is what you must become — otherwise everything is void. How can I, a man not yet thirty, take out with me to India a girl of less than twenty years of age — unless she happens to be married to me?

Jane How can you not?

St John How can we be forever together — and unwed?

Jane But I have no more love for you than you have for me!

St John Enough of love would follow after we were married, Jane, I promise you, to prove to both of us what we had done was right. You were formed to serve God — not for love.

Jane No. No, St John! I will not marry you and I beg you not to press me further on this subject.

St John But I must. I have to. I believe it to be my duty.

Jane And I believe that I am bounden by a stronger cord than duty.

St John I know where your heart looks, Jane, and to what it clings to still.

You cannot forget your Edward Rochester, can you? Do you intend to go and find him?

Jane I must. I have to know what has become of him.

St John I had thought I had recognized in you one of God's children. It only remains for me then to remember you in my prayers and to entreat God on your behalf and in all earnestness, that you may not become a castaway. I cannot give you up to perdition, "He that overcometh shall inherit all things." If I listened to human pride, Jane, I should not mention marriage to you further — but I do listen to duty — and do all things to the glory of God.

Jane makes no move as he gathers her to him with one arm while he puts his other hand, firmly, on top of her head

Resolve — repent, Jane, while there is time left still. God give you the strength to choose that path which is the right one. Could you decide now?

Jane I could decide, if I were but certain — if I could be sure that it was God's will that I should marry you here and now — come afterwards what would.

St John My prayers are heard!

He releases Jane and she takes a step backwards, away from him. The evening is drifting towards night. Jane turns her face to heaven

Jane Show me! Show me the path!

A soft wind soughs across the moorland and Jane shudders with expectancy

St John What is it? What can you hear? What do you see?

Then, on the wind, with Jane we can just make out a voice crying out to her across the miles that separate her from Rochester — wildly, eerily, urgently

Rochester (*off*) Jane! Jane! Jane!

Jane Oh God! What is it? I am coming! Wait for me! Where are you?

Then, on the wind, almost as if in echo, Rochester's voice cries out again, but even fainter than before

Rochester (*off*) Where are you... ?

As Jane sets off, urgently and in the direction from which the voice came, St John watches her go, his hands clasped head-high, half in fear of his own safety, half in plea for Jane's spiritual salvation

Scene 10

Outside Thornfield Hall

Six Narrators move on, in phalanx, as urgently as Jane strode off

First Narrator Once more on the road to Thornfield more than a day past.
Second Narrator How fast I walked, how I even ran sometimes.
Third Narrator Another field crossed, a lane threaded ——
Fourth Narrator — and there were the courtyard walls — the rookery still hid, the house itself.
Fifth Narrator I determined to view it from the front where its bold battlements will strike the eye at once ——
Sixth Narrator — and where I can single out my master's very window.
First Narrator Perhaps he will be standing at it — could I but see him.
Second Narrator Surely, in that case, I should not be so mad as to run towards him.
Third Narrator I cannot tell.
Fourth Narrator And if I did——
Fifth Narrator —what then?
Sixth Narrator God bless him, what then?
First Narrator I looked with hesitant joy towards the stately house.
Second Narrator I saw a blackened ruin ——
Third Narrator —— a burnt out shell — the silence of death about it.
Fourth Narrator The solitude of a lonesome wild ——

As the Narrators withdraw, Jane enters aghast, as an elderly Builder enters with a cart and who, during the following, salvages rubble

Jane How did it happen? When?

Builder Harvest time. You never saw naught like it. The fire caught hold at midnight — th'ouse — th'furniture — the lot. It was a fine place, Thornfield Hall.

Jane I lived here once.

Builder That makes two of us. I was headgroom here — till I moved across the valley and took up dry-stone walling — that was after they buried the master.

Jane Is Mr Rochester dead?

Builder Not this one isn't. This one's father. The old Mr Rochester.

Jane Then Edward Rochester's alive? Praise God! Does he live here still?

Builder It were a madwoman he kept upstairs, by all accounts as started it. She ended up on t' roof, shouting and screaming, waving her arms about. Her hair caught fire at the death afore she chucked herself off. Smashed to naught on the cobblestones.

Jane But Mr Rochester is well?

Builder If you can call it well — he harmed himself in trying to save the madwoman. Got up as far as the roof, though God knows how, afore the flames damn near roasted him and drove him back.

Jane He is in England?

Builder Oh, ay. He's in England. He can't get out of England. He's a fixture. He lost the sight of both his eyes — and crippled his self. There's a servant lass stopped on to cook and clean and that for him. He's blind as a bat.

Jane Where's his house?

Builder The very last one on t'other side of the village. The one with the apple-trees in t' front garden.

Jane (*moving to leave, then pausing*) There was a little girl — his ward?

Builder She's off at school, in France.

As Jane moves off again, he calls after her

There's a big missel-barn one end — you can't mistake it!

As Jane hurries off in one direction, the Builder pushes his cart off in another, as we go to:

SCENE 11

The Garden, Ferndean

A chair has been brought out from the house and is positioned, c

It is now twilight and Rochester enters, slowly, his hand on Leah's shoulder

Jane enters downstage and watches as Leah, who is carrying a tray containing a lit candle and a glass of water, guides Rochester to the chair

Rochester's hands move over the chair, establishing its familiar contours. He sits and Leah moves away. Jane steps out in front of Leah, putting a finger to her lips

Leah (*whispering*) Is it really you, miss? Come at this late hour?
Jane I'll take it to him.

Jane lifts the candle and the glass of water off the tray

Leah He always has a candle when it's dark — even though it's not a bit of use to him.

Leah moves off into the house

Jane crosses towards Rochester, placing the candle on the ground

Rochester Give me the water, Leah.

Jane puts the glass to his lips and he drinks a little

This is Leah, is it not?
Jane Leah is back inside the house.
Rochester Who is this? Who is this? Answer me — speak again.
Jane Will you have a little more water, Edward?
Rochester Who is it? What is it? Who speaks? (*His hand moves along her arm*) Is it Jane? What is it? This is her shape — this is her size ...

Jane And this is her voice. She is all here: her heart too.
Rochester Jane Eyre! Jane Eyre!
Jane I am come back to you.

She kisses his sightless eyes and then his forehead

Rochester It is you. And do you not lie dead in some ditch, under some stream? And are you not a pining outcast amongst strangers?
Jane No, sir! I am an independent woman now.
Rochester Independent? What do you mean?
Jane My uncle in Madeira is dead and he has left me an inheritance. I am my own mistress.
Rochester And I have not been lucky. (*He draws his arm, which is severed below the elbow, out of his sleeve*) On this arm I have neither hand nor nails. It is a stump — a ghastly sight. Don't you think so, Jane?
Jane It is a pity to see it. And pity to see your eyes — and the scar of fire on your forehead. And the worst of it is, one is in danger of loving you too well for all this. Have you a pocket-comb about you, sir?
Rochester What for, Jane?
Jane To comb out this shaggy black mane. I find you rather alarming when I examine you at close hand.
Rochester Am I hideous, Jane?
Jane Very, sir. You always were, you know.
Rochester Humph! The wickedness has not been taken out of you, wherever you have been.
Jane Yet I have been with good people. Far better than you — a hundred times better people.
Rochester Who the deuce have you been with?
Jane Later, later. Another time. None that you need be jealous of. Oh, if you knew how much I do love you, you would be proud and content. All my heart is yours, sir. It belongs to you.

Rochester kisses her hand, then turns his face away, consumed by grief

Rochester I am no better than the chestnut tree that was struck down by lightning at Thornfield. And what right would that old shell have to ask a budding woodbine to cover its rotting bark with freshness?
Jane You are no old shell, sir. No rotting tree. You are green and vigorous. Plants will spring up about your roots, whether or not you ask them,

because they take delight in your bountiful shadow — and, as they grow, they will lean towards you, and wind round you, because they will take their strength from you.

Rochester Are we friends, Jane?

Jane We are, we are.

Rochester Ah, Jane! But I want a wife.

Jane Do you, sir?

Rochester Yes. It is unwelcome news?

Jane That depends on circumstances, sir. On your choice.

Rochester Which you shall make for me, Jane. I will abide by your decision.

Jane Choose then, sir — her who loves you best.

Rochester I will choose, at least, her I love best. (*He lowers himself off the chair and kneels at her feet*) Jane, will you marry me?

Jane (*kneeling to join him*) Yes, sir.

Rochester A poor blind man, whom you will have to lead about by the hand.

Jane Yes, sir.

Rochester A crippled man, twenty years older than you, whom you will have to wait on, hand and foot?

Jane Yes, sir.

Rochester Truly, Jane?

Jane Most truly, sir.

They embrace

Rochester (*embracing Jane*) Oh my darling, God bless you and reward you!

Jane Sir, if ever I did a good deed in my life — if ever I thought a good thought — if ever I prayed a true and righteous prayer — if ever I wished a righteous wish — I am rewarded now. To the finest fibre of my nature, sir.

Rochester (*unfastening his watch and giving it to her*) What time is it?

Jane Half-past seven o'clock.

She tries to give it back to him but he pushes it away

Rochester Fasten it in your girdle, Jane, and keep it henceforward.

Jane rises then helps him to his feet

Jane The sun has gone down — but it has dried up all the raindrops. The evening breeze is warm. Shall we go for a walk?

He nods. She puts his arm around her shoulder and they start to move off, slowly

How fitting, sir, that I am so much lower in stature than yourself — I can serve both as your prop and as your guide.

Then, as they are about to move off together, they pause — she gazes, slowly, around the audience, before informing them

I married him.

The Lights fade to Black-out

FURNITURE AND PROPERTY LIST

Garter for **Miss Abbott**
Book for **Brocklehurst**
Small trunk for **Bessie**
Lantern for **Bessie**
Child-size chairs
Blackboard
Slate for **Jane**
Slates for **School children**
Tea
A tray for **Barbara**. *On it*: bread and butter, two cups and saucers
Small package of seed-cake
Small iron-bound bed covered with light blankets
Candles
Lilies for **Girls**
Trunk for **Jane**
Scrap of paper for **Bessie**
Book for **Adele**
Supper tray for **Leah**
Water-jug
Soiled towel
Warming-pans
Bed linen
Chairs
Footstools
Small table
Brandy decanter
Two glasses
Tray
Candelabra
Doll for **Adele**
Piano with sheet music
Stick for **Rochester**
Travel rug
Portfolio of water colour painting and pencil drawings
Pencils
Rush torch for **Bertha**
Tray of food for **Grace Poole**
Glasses of wine for **Gorstone Guests**
Luggage for **Servants**
Cushion for **Mary**
Box of expensive chocolates for **Lord Ingram**

Candlestick
Pistol for **Lord Ingram**
Bowl of water, bandages and sponge for **Jane**
Freshly picked flowers for **Mrs Fairfax**
Several brace of game for **John**
Dress box for **Leah**. *In it*: wedding dress
Vase for **Kitty**
Small substitute veil for **Leah**
Couple of hairpins for **Leah**
Pair of benches
Large, free-standing ornate candlesticks
Folder containing official looking document
Wedding gifts
Fragment of cloth for **Bertha Mason**
Small pile of crisply ironed white garments
A locket for a **Narrator**
A ring for a **Narrator**
Pearl necklace for **Jane**
Small purse containing some coins for a **Narrator**
Large wicker-basket containing breadcakes
Small lace-edged handkerchief for **Jane**
Scrap of food for **Country Girl**
Four upright chairs
Hymn books for **Diana, Mary** and **Hannah**
A book for **John**
Small breadcake
Tea things for **Diana** and **Mary**
Tablecloth for **Hannah**
Christmas cake, cheeses, hot punch, pastries *etc*. for **Hannah**
Rubble
Cart
Pocket watch for **Rochester**

LIGHTING PLOT

Property fitting required: chandelier with lit candles
Various interior and exterior settings

ACT I
To open: Full general lighting

Cue 1   **Narrators** : "... and cutting it."   (Page 2)
          Fade and bring up on Scene 1

Cue 2   **The sound of wind**   (Page 3)
          Fade and bring up on Scene 2

Cue 3   **Jane** storms out of the room   (Page 5)
          Fade and bring up lights on two of the **Narrators** *on the gallery*

Cue 4   **First Narrator**: "... the only person yet risen."   (Page 5)
          Bring up lights on Scene 3

Cue 5   **The Groom** puts his arm around **Bessie's** waist   (Page 6)
          Fade and bring up lights on the **Narrators** *on the gallery*

Cue 6   **Second Narrator**: " ... and 'shameful'"   (Page 7)
          Bring up lights on Scene 4

Cue 7   **Jane**: "I was suddenly borne up!"   (Page 9)
          Fade on **Jane** *and bring up lights on* **Narrators** *about the stage*

Cue 8   **Sixth Narrator**: "Helen Burns was near."   (Page 10)
          Bring up lights on **Jane** *on the floor*

Cue 9   **Second Narrator**: " ... reached her apartment."   (Page 10)
          Fade and bring up lights on Scene 5

Cue 10 **Miss Temple** serves the tea   (Page 12)
          Fade on the Scene 5 and bring up lights on another area of the stage

Cue 11 **Jane and Helen** sleep   (Page 14)
          Fade and bring up lights to morning effect

Cue 12 **The Girls** enter, each carrying a single lily   (Page 15)
          Bring up lights to day effect

Cue 13   The Bride and Groom go off, hand in hand   (Page 15)
            Fade on the wedding scene. Snap on spot on Mrs Fairfax

Cue 14   Mrs Fairfax: "... character and competency — "   (Page 15)
            Bring up lights on Scene 8

Cue 15   Mrs Fairfax: " ... near Millcote, West Yorkshire..."   (Page 16)
            Fade on Mrs Fairfax

Cue 16   Jane and Bessie move downstage   (Page 18)
            Bring up lights on Scene 9

Cue 17   Jane moves to exit. The soughing of the moorland wind   (Page 21)
            Fade and bring up lights on Scene 10

Cue 18   As Scene 10 opens   (Page 21)
            Bring up moonlight effect. Lightning

Cue 19   Jane assists Rochester to hobble off stage   (Page 22)
            Fade and come up as night-time effect

Cue 20   Jane takes off her shawl and bonnet   (Page 24)
            Fade lights momentarily and come up again on the same scene

Cue 21   Mrs Fairfax: " ...matters that trouble him."   (Page 26)
            Fade and bring up lights on four Narrators on the gallery

Cue 22   Fourth Narrator: " ... to return those visits."   (Page 26)
            Fade on the Narrators and come up on Scene 12

Cue 23   The ripple of maniacal laughter   (Page 30)
            Cross-fade to dim lighting on the gallery

Cue 24   Bertha Mason hastens in and out of view   (Page 30)
            Fade on the gallery and bring up lights on Scene 13

Cue 25   To open Scene 13   (Page 30)
            Flickering flame effect behind white muslin curtain

Cue 26   Jane stamps out fire   (Page 30)
            Cut flame effect

Cue 27   Rochester and Mrs Fairfax hold each other's glance   (Page 32)
            Fade and bring up lights on Scene 14

Cue 28   **Mrs Fairfax** peers out over the gallery   (Page 33)
          Jane *and* **Mrs Fairfax** *are held in the spot*

Cue 29   **Mrs Fairfax**: " ... denying that she was queen..."   (Page 34)
          Bring up lights on Scene 15

Cue 30   **Mrs Fairfax**: " ... best match in the county."   (Page 34)
          Fade spot on the gallery

Cue 31   **Second Guest**: "...matches are made every day."   (Page 35)
          Fade and snap on spot on Jane

Cue 32   **Jane**: " ... plain-face household servant."   (Page 35)
          Snap off spot on Jane and bring up on Scene 16

Cue 33   **Rochester and Blanche** move into the house   (Page 37)
          Fade and bring up lights on Scene 17

Cue 34   **Rochester**: "...heard a carriage in the drive."   (Page 39)
          Fade lights

*Cue*35   **Rochester**: "This way."   (Page 39)
          *Bring up lights slowly on the drawing-room and the group
            at the piano*

Cue 36   A scream, somewhere in the house   (Page 41)
          Fade on drawing-room but increase to semi-darkness on Scene 18

Cue 37   **Narrator**: " ... wall bordering the orchard."   (Page 44)
          Fade and bring up lights immediately on Scene 19

Cue 38   **Rochester** kisses **Jane** on the mouth. She responds   (Page 46)
          Fade lights

Cue 39   The sound of mocking laughter   (Page 46)
          Bring up lights on impending wedding scene downstage

Cue 40   **Mrs Fairfax and Kitty** exit   (Page 47)
          Fade and bring up lights on Scene 20

Cue 41   **Jane** gets into bed   (Page 49)
          Dim lights

Cue 42   **Jane** screams   (Page 49)
              Black-out

ACT II

To open: Early morning effect

Cue 43   Rochester has led **Jane** off stage   (Page 55)
              Fade lights. Snap on spot on two **Narrators** *on the gallery*

Cue 44   Fourth Narrator: " — all was still."   (Page 55)
              Fade and bring up lights on Scene 2

Cue 45   Second Narrator: " ... ceiling by a chain."   (Page 58)
              Fade and bring up lights on Scene 3

Cue 46   To open SCENE 3   (Page 58)
              *Open in darkness. Fireglow. Gradually bring up sufficient
                  light to make out the figure of* **Grace Poole**

Cue 47   Jane crosses downstage   (Page 59)
              Fade lights on **Grace Poole** *and* **Bertha Mason**

Cue 48   **Jane**: "My hopes are dead."   (Page 60)
              Bring up lights on Scene 4

Cue 49   Jane (*off*): "Farewell, Mr Rochester—"   (Page 64)
              Fade and bring up lights on Scene 5

Cue 50   **Jane**: " He has not slept at all."   (Page 66)
              Spot comes up slowly on **Rochester**

Cue 51   **Jane**: " But that I must not do."   (Page 66)
              Bring up lights slowly to establish full morning light

Cue 52   **Rochester**: " Come back to me!"   (Page 67)
              Fade lights on **Rochester**

Cue 53   Jane sinks to the ground   (Page 67)
              Fade and bring up lights on **Jane** *and the* **Narrators**

Cue 54   St John: " ... footsteps to our door!"   (Page 71)
              Fade lights

Cue 55   **Narrator: "I thanked God — exhausted, I slept."**   (Page 71)
          Bring up lights on previous scene

Cue 56   **Mary and Diana embrace Jane**   (Page 75)
          Fade on Rivers' parlour and bring up lights on Scene 7

Cue 57   **Jane: " ... and Alice will collect them in. "**   (Page 75)
          Fade on the school-room but hold Jane in a spot

Cue 58   **Jane: " ...here in the heart of England —-?**   (Page 76)
          Bring up lights on school-room

Cue 59   **Jane: " I know exactly what I mean to do ..."**   (Page 81)
          Fade and bring up lights on Scene 8

Cue 60   **Carol-singers reach the end of their first chord**   (Page 83)
          Fade and bring up sunny evening effect on Scene 9

Cue 61   **St John releases Jane and she takes a step backwards**   (Page 85)
          Slow fade to night-effect

Cue 62   **To open SCENE 10**   (Page 86)
          Full general lighting

Cue 63   **To open SCENE 11**   (Page 88)
          Bring down lights to a twilight effect

Cue 64   **Jane: "I married him."**   (Page 91)
          Fade to black-out

EFFECTS PLOT

ACT I

ACT II

THE POOR ORPHAN CHILD.

Music by
Stephen Warbeck.

Milton Keynes UK
Ingram Content Group UK Ltd.
UKHW022013120124
435937UK00012B/643